Building E-commerce Sites with VirtueMart Cookbook

Over 90 recipes to help you build an attractive, profitable, and fully-featured e-commerce store with VirtueMart

John Horton

[PACKT] open source*

PUBLISHING   community experience distilled

BIRMINGHAM - MUMBAI

Building E-commerce Sites with VirtueMart Cookbook

First published: June 2013

Production Reference: 1170613

Published by Packt Publishing Ltd.
Livery Place
35 Livery Street
Birmingham B3 2PB, UK.

ISBN 978-1-78216-208-7

www.packtpub.com

Cover Image by Gorkee Bhardwaj (afterglowpictures@gmail.com)

Credits

Author
John Horton

Reviewers
Jordi Català Castillo

Jörgen Hübner

Sabuj Kumar Kundu

Kelvyn Sheppard

Acquisition Editors
Andrew Duckworth

Sam Birch

Lead Technical Editor
Mayur Hule

Technical Editors
Athira Laji

Anita Nayak

Zafeer Rais

Sonali Vernekar

Project Coordinator
Shiksha Chaturvedi

Proofreaders
Amy Guest

Bernadette Watkins

Indexer
Monica Ajmera Mehta

Production Coordinator
Nitesh Thakur

Cover Work
Nitesh Thakur

About the Author

John Horton spends his working hours helping people make their websites/apps/e-commerce enterprises successful through his business, www.HadronWebDesign.com.

He also encourages the pursuit of mathematics through the free Android app, MathLegends which is available on www.MathLegends.com.

In his spare time he likes shooting zombies with his two sons.

For Jo, Jack, and James.

About the Reviewers

Jordi Catà Castillo is a software engineer with more than 12 years of experience in free software, focused on web development with technologies such as PHP, Joomla, Symfony2, and Prestashop.

His graduation project, titled "Interactive Architectonic Walkthrough" was awarded the Best Graduation Project of the University of Girona.

At the beginning of his career, Jordi was involved with the investigation of Graphical Computing in the development of new illumination techniques for state-of-the-art videogames through graphical engines such as Crystal Space and Ogre3D. He has also collaborated in the publication of several technical papers and the book *ShadersX5*.

In 2005, he formed his own company (`dunlock.com` and `webactualizable.com`), specializing in web development and Joomla!. In 2010 he joined forces with another partner to create `Arambee.com`.

With regards to Joomla! and Virtuemart, Jordi has worked on different kinds of projects, from corporative websites to the integration of Joomla! with ERP and CRM via web services, and has developed several extensions for customers.

Jordi has participated as a speaker in several conferences on Joomla! and PHP development in Spain, such as the *Joomla! Days Spain* (2009: co-organizer and speaker in 2010, 2012), the *PHPConference*, and the *Free Software Talks*.

Jordi is a part of different entrepreneurship initiatives in Spain such as `Iniciador.com` (co-organizer in Barcelona from 2008 to 2012, co-organizer in Girona since 2012) and the *Junior Chamber International* of Girona.

Jörgen Hübner was born in Uppsala, near Stockholm, in 1961 and holds a degree in mechanical engineering. He has more than 20 years of experience in the development and design of microcontroller-based products. He is responsible for almost all of the development steps, schematic design, PCB layout, software design, programming in C, and also design of testing procedures for the finished products. He holds a black belt in Judo and has been active in Judo for more than 30 years, 15 years of these as an instructor. Besides this he also likes photography.

He runs his own web shop `www.kreativfotografi.se` selling camera accessories. The web shop is of course powered by Joomla! and Virtuemart.

Kelvyn Sheppard first learned the elements of computer programming around 1975 while working as a biomedical scientist in the UK National Health Service. Following a move to the English Lake district, he set up his first website development business in 1996 and now owns and manages Jenkin Hill Internet which provides website development services and consultancy.

Having built an e-commerce website in 2007 using an early version of VirtueMart, Kelvyn became interested in the development of the component and became a moderator on the VirtueMart support forum in 2009. Working with the VM development team as a writer and tester, he now manages the busy support forum, all in his spare time and in a voluntary capacity.

Sabuj Kumar Kundu is the founder and CEO of Codeboxr. He has almost 7 years of experience in the IT field.

The website `Manchumahara.com` with the tag line "let's start again..." is his personal blog site where he writes about technology, spirituality, and poems.

Codeboxr is a web service start-up company (founded in 2011) revolving around organic ideas and meeting demands of our clients with advanced solutions for a social and friendly web experience. The company is very enthusiastic about social media, its potential, and how to better integrate it within sites that want meaningful engagement with their visitors and customers. It builds extensions for industry leading content management systems (such as Joomla!, Drupal, and WordPress) to make web2.0 more socially integrated.

I would like to thank myself as I managed time to review this book.

www.PacktPub.com

Support files, eBooks, discount offers and more

You might want to visit www.PacktPub.com for support files and downloads related to your book.

Did you know that Packt offers eBook versions of every book published, with PDF and ePub files available? You can upgrade to the eBook version at www.PacktPub.com and as a print book customer, you are entitled to a discount on the eBook copy. Get in touch with us at service@packtpub.com for more details.

At www.PacktPub.com, you can also read a collection of free technical articles, sign up for a range of free newsletters and receive exclusive discounts and offers on Packt books and eBooks.

http://PacktLib.PacktPub.com

Do you need instant solutions to your IT questions? PacktLib is Packt's online digital book library. Here, you can access, read and search across Packt's entire library of books.

Why Subscribe?

- Fully searchable across every book published by Packt
- Copy and paste, print and bookmark content
- On demand and accessible via web browser

Free Access for Packt account holders

If you have an account with Packt at www.PacktPub.com, you can use this to access PacktLib today and view nine entirely free books. Simply use your login credentials for immediate access.

Table of Contents

Preface

Welcome to *Building E-commerce Sites with VirtueMart Cookbook*. The next few pages will help you decide if Joomla!, VirtueMart, and this book can help you succeed with your latest online store or client. If you are a seasoned VirtueMart pro, you can skip a couple of paragraphs and jump to the section *Who this book is for* because you probably already realize the potential. But if you are a relative newcomer to Joomla!, VirtueMart or e-commerce, then you have a big opportunity and I urge you to find out more.

VirtueMart and Joomla!

Joomla! is huge. I was browsing their forums the other day and I noticed they now have over 600,000 members. According to their own statistics they now have 35 million core downloads and thousands of different extensions. It would be a fairly awkward argument to not agree that Joomla! is the foremost, one of the best-featured, and one of the most extendable CMS there is!

In the recent past however there has been criticism of the Joomla! e-commerce options. It is still true that the e-commerce options are far from perfect. But now with the latest version of VirtueMart, alongside a growing list of high-quality extensions and a vast array of other Joomla!/e-commerce options to fill the occasional VirtueMart void; Joomla! users and developers are faced with a huge opportunity! To offer the best CMS bar none, integrated with just about any e-commerce feature imaginable. Oh, and most of it is free!

Exploring this opportunity is the purpose of the recipes in this book.

What this book covers

Chapter 1, Setting Up Shop covers the installation of Joomla! and VirtueMart as well as the configuration of the basic and essential options.

Chapter 2, Merchandising VirtueMart introduces the addition of our products and product categories as well as some advanced features via VirtueMart's custom fields.

Chapter 3, Shipping and Taxes covers how to offer efficient and easy-to understand shipping and tax options to suit a number of different scenarios, the day our store can be unleashed on the public.

Chapter 4, Making Your Store Look Amazing explains some of the template options available in Joomla!/VirtueMart, including pre-built frameworks to simple but the powerful GUI template creation software.

Chapter 5, Going Live explains what to do about handling orders, refunds, and so on, when our VirtueMart store goes live.

Chapter 6, Killer SEO explains how to make use of all the Joomla! and VirtueMart SEO features, in a crowded web, to make sure that our new store is found by the search engines.

Chapter 7, Extending Joomla! and VirtueMart covers a number of ways to get more out of Joomla! and VirtueMart to add exciting features to our shop. Want to add an affiliate campaign, detect which country your customers come from, or add PHP and JavaScript to your site content? Then this chapter is for you.

Chapter 8, VirtueMart Alternatives explains how VirtueMart does not suit every occasion. If you want to have simple product sales from articles, open a downloads store or don't mind paying to get even more features than VirtueMart, then this chapter is the one to read.

Chapter 9, Blueprint – Making an Android App out of Your Site Content explains how apps are big business and all the big businesses have an app. This blueprint chapter will take you one recipe at a time towards wrapping your site in an Android app and publishing it on Google Play.

Appendix, Joomla! and VirtueMart Resources introduces some additional resources for your reference.

What you need for this book

A modern Linux, Mac, or Windows computer. All the recipes have been thoroughly tried and tested on a Windows 7 PC but should cause no trouble to the moderately experienced Linux/Mac user to perform on their machines.

Similarly, although all of the recipes have been tried and tested on the Joomla! recommended Rochen hosting service, they could easily be completed on any other host that meets the required specifications or a self-hosted WAMP or LAMP setup.

The hosting requirements are as follows:

- PHP v5.2.17
- MySQL 5.04+
- Apache 2.x

It would also be neat if you installed a good FTP client like FileZilla for transferring Joomla!, VirtueMart and many other interesting things we will be talking about, onto your Web server. That's it!

Who this book is for

This book is for readers of all levels who want to setup an e-commerce store with Joomla!. The guides and tutorials are set out as self-contained recipes so that readers who are new to Joomla! or VirtueMart can start off with the very basics of setting up their new store.

There are also many, more advanced tutorials such as configuring the more awkward aspects of VirtueMart or making your site into an Android app. These would be better suited for the existing VirtueMart administrators. However, it is hoped that the less experienced reader could be prepared for these more advanced recipes by reading and implementing the easier ones first.

Although the recipes start at an elementary level in terms of Joomla! and VirtueMart knowledge, it is assumed that the reader will have a good grasp of basic PC skills and a reasonable understanding of how to navigate around the control panel of their chosen hosting solution.

Conventions

In this book, you will find a number of styles of text that distinguish between different kinds of information. Here are some examples of these styles, and an explanation of their meaning.

Code words in text are shown as follows: "We can include other contexts through the use of the include directive".

A block of code is set as follows:

```
<!-- Slideshow 1 -->
    <ul class="rslides" id="slider1">
      <li><img src="images/1.jpg" alt=""></li>
      <li><img src="images/2.jpg" alt=""></li>
      <li><img src="images/3.jpg" alt=""></li>
    </ul>
```

When we wish to draw your attention to a particular part of a code block, the relevant lines or items are set in bold:

```
<!-- Slideshow 1 -->
    <ul class="rslides" id="slider1">
      <li><img src="images/1.jpg" alt=""></li>
      <li><img src="images/2.jpg" alt=""></li>
      <li><img src="images/3.jpg" alt=""></li>
    </ul>
```

New terms and **important words** are shown in bold. Words that you see on the screen, in menus or dialog boxes for example, appear in the text like this: "clicking the **Next** button moves you to the next screen".

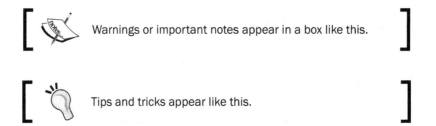

Warnings or important notes appear in a box like this.

Tips and tricks appear like this.

Reader feedback

Feedback from our readers is always welcome. Let us know what you think about this book—what you liked or may have disliked. Reader feedback is important for us to develop titles that you really get the most out of.

To send us general feedback, simply send an e-mail to feedback@packtpub.com, and mention the book title via the subject of your message.

If there is a book that you need and would like to see us publish, please send us a note in the **SUGGEST A TITLE** form on www.packtpub.com or e-mail suggest@packtpub.com.

If there is a topic that you have expertise in and you are interested in either writing or contributing to a book, see our author guide on www.packtpub.com/authors.

Customer support

Now that you are the proud owner of a Packt book, we have a number of things to help you to get the most from your purchase.

Downloading the example code

You can download the example code files for all Packt books you have purchased from your account at http://www.PacktPub.com. If you purchased this book elsewhere, you can visit http://www.PacktPub.com/support and register to have the files e-mailed directly to you.

Errata

Although we have taken every care to ensure the accuracy of our content, mistakes do happen. If you find a mistake in one of our books—maybe a mistake in the text or the code—we would be grateful if you would report this to us. By doing so, you can save other readers from frustration and help us improve subsequent versions of this book. If you find any errata, please report them by visiting `http://www.packtpub.com/support`, selecting your book, clicking on the **errata submission form** link, and entering the details of your errata. Once your errata are verified, your submission will be accepted and the errata will be uploaded on our website, or added to any list of existing errata, under the Errata section of that title. Any existing errata can be viewed by selecting your title from `http://www.packtpub.com/support`.

Piracy

Piracy of copyright material on the Internet is an ongoing problem across all media. At Packt, we take the protection of our copyright and licenses very seriously. If you come across any illegal copies of our works, in any form, on the Internet, please provide us with the location address or website name immediately so that we can pursue a remedy.

Please contact us at `copyright@packtpub.com` with a link to the suspected pirated material.

We appreciate your help in protecting our authors, and our ability to bring you valuable content.

Questions

You can contact us at `questions@packtpub.com` if you are having a problem with any aspect of the book, and we will do our best to address it.

1
Setting Up Shop

In this chapter we will cover:

- ▸ Installing Joomla! 2.5 in your web space
- ▸ Increasing the Joomla! session lifetime
- ▸ Installing VirtueMart and the core add-ons
- ▸ Familiarizing yourself with VirtueMart
- ▸ Removing the VirtueMart AIO component
- ▸ Creating a link to our store
- ▸ Removing the currency not defined error
- ▸ Filling out the company information section
- ▸ Fixing the safe path warning
- ▸ Setting up your company identity in VirtueMart
- ▸ Creating a menu for your must-have information
- ▸ Displaying the core VirtueMart menus

Introduction

Welcome to *Setting Up Shop*. As the name suggests, by the end of this chapter you will have a working **Joomla!**/**VirtueMart** installation, with some core e-commerce features such as a shopping cart, product search, and fully functioning backend control panel.

The first step is to install Joomla! itself, then VirtueMart and its core components, and then we move on to the first steps of configuration of the VirtueMart. Then we will create the must-have e-commerce pages such as About us. Next we create a custom menu to link to the must-have pages that we just created, and finish up by arranging some core e-commerce modules such as a shopping cart.

Let's not waste any time. If you have your Joomla! site already, you can skip this recipe. If you haven't got one, you will in about 10 minutes.

Installing Joomla! 2.5 in your web space

Let's get started by downloading and installing Joomla!

Getting ready

Head on over to www.joomla.org. Click on the **Download** button and grab a copy of **Joomla! 2.5** and place the ZIP file on your desktop. Fire up **FileZilla** and make ready a connection to your web space where your new VirtueMart store will be "set up." If you have never done this before, follow the quick guide.

Connecting to your web host with FileZilla

This is really easy. Perform the following steps:

1. Run FileZilla.
2. Navigate to **File | Site Manager | New Site**.
3. Enter the details shown in the following table:

Field	Value
Host	The FTP web address supplied by your host. Often this is the same as your website URL.
Logon type	Normal.
User	Your username supplied by your web hosting company.
Password	Your password supplied by the web hosting company.

The other values are usually fine as they are.

4. Click on **Connect**.

Your web space is on the right of the FileZilla window and your computer is on the left. You can move files about in FileZilla in a manner similar to your operating system. Browse to the folders you require on the left and right. Then do drag-and-drop between them as shown in the following screenshot:

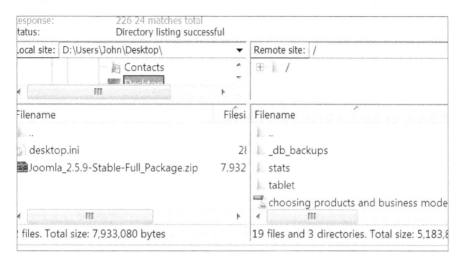

Have your details to hand

Log in to your web hosting control panel. You will need a MySQL database and this will need to be created in your control panel. When you have done so, here will most likely be a database details screen where you can grab the details ready for the installation of your Joomla! site, namely **Database name**, **Username**, **Password**, **Hostname**, and **Database type**, usually **MySQLi**.

How to do it...

Here it is in 12 simple steps and about as many minutes to a functioning Joomla! site:

1. Using FileZilla, drag the file `Joomla_2.5.x-Stable-Full_Package.zip` from your desktop to your web space pointed to by your web store URL. This should ideally take about two minutes, but if you have a slow internet connection (like mine), then you might like to grab a cup of tea, and perhaps a walk in the park.

2. In your web hosts file manager find the file you just uploaded and unzip it.

3. In your web browser go to the home URL of your new site, `www.yoursite.com`. You will see the following screenshot:

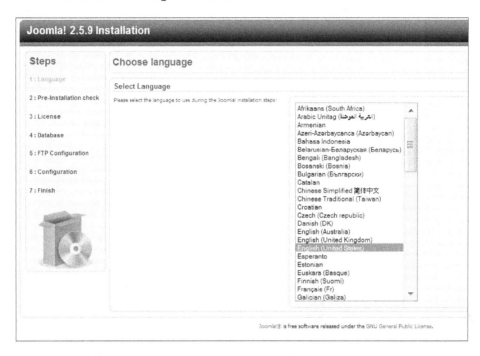

4. Choose your language such as **English (United States)** from the list and click on the **Next** button in the top-right corner. Now we have the following screenshot:

If you have any (**No**) indicators in the top box, then there is an incompatibility between Joomla! and your web hosts. You will need to contact your web host to fix the problem. If you have any (**On/Off**) indicators you can proceed but make a note of the warning and research its potential implications.

5. When you're ready to proceed, click on the **Next** button.

6. The next screen asks you to agree to the **GNU General Public License**. The license allows you to do almost anything with Joomla! for free! What's not to agree about? Click on the **Next** button again.

7. On the next screen we need to fill out our database information from our web hosts. The stuff we got ready earlier. In the following screenshot, enter your database details that we prepared in the *Getting ready* section. For **Database Type** choose **Mysqli**. Click on **Next**. Refer to the following screenshot:

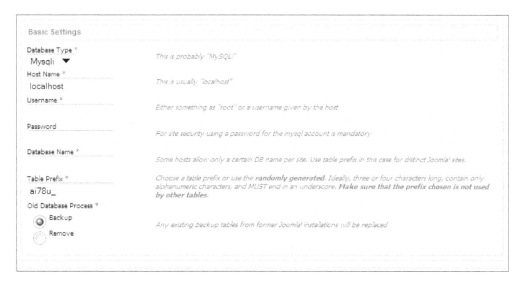

8. The next screen is usually left blank as it is not needed. Click on **Next**.

9. Nearly there. Choose a **Site name**, **Username**, and **Password**. Enter your e-mail address for the Joomla! system to use, to contact you.

 If you are new to Joomla! it could be useful to click on the **Install sample data** button. These are some dummy articles and categories that flesh out your new site. It makes it easier to click around and explore the admin control panel to learn what is going on. As we will cover very little (except VirtueMart essential) Joomla! specific stuff, it is probably a good idea to do this if you are new to this.

10. Click on **Next**.

11. Click on **Next** once again.

12. Click on the **Remove installation folder** button to remove the installation folder and prevent someone from reinstalling over all your hard work.

> **PLEASE REMEMBER TO COMPLETELY
> REMOVE THE INSTALLATION FOLDER.**
> You will not be able to proceed beyond this point until the installation directory
> has been removed. This is a security feature of Joomla!.
>
> Remove installation folder

Go and explore your new Joomla! control panel and your site by clicking on the appropriate buttons in the top right.

How it works...

So what just happened there was that we ran the Joomla! install. In the process we gave the system everything it needs to create a site and the admin features needed to develop it. Now, we are almost done as the next step is to install the VirtueMart component to turn our world beating CMS into an e-commerce selling machine.

Increasing the Joomla! session lifetime

Some of the recipes we undertake will often mean that we start the work in some part of the Joomla! control panel and then leave it partly done while reading further or perhaps gathering information elsewhere. Joomla!, in an effort to be helpful and secure, will log us out after 15 minutes.

Getting ready

I would suggest that changing this session lifetime to 60 minutes is sufficient to virtually always avoid entering loads of data, only to have that data wiped because we hadn't saved it yet and Joomla! logged us out.

How to do it...

Log in to your Joomla! control panel using the username and password you chose in the first recipe:

1. Now from the Joomla! drop-down menu navigate to **Site | Global Configuration**, then find this area on the right-hand side of the screen.

2. Now simply change the **15** in the **Session Lifetime** box to 60 and click on **Save** in the top right.

How it works...

The change of the session lifetime to 60 changes an entry in the Joomla! configuration settings and prevents the system from logging us out after 15 minutes of inactivity. That period is now 60 minutes and we are much less likely to lose some configuration settings before we had a chance to click on **Save**.

 It is still possible to lose work and when it does happen because we have increased the session lifetime it is possible that the amount of work we lose could be greater than before! So save regularly when prompted and whenever you have some settings or awkward configurations in a form that is unsaved.

Installing VirtueMart and the core add-ons

After this super quick, complexity free recipe, you will have a new option in your Joomla! components menu, that is VirtueMart. Clicking on the VirtueMart component link will open up a wealth of configuration and settings comparable to many standalone shopping cart systems.

Getting ready

Let's get the files necessary to do the installation. Head over to www.virtuemart.net and click on the **Download** tab. Download the latest stable version available. Got it? Let's go.

How to do it...

Let's install VirtueMart:

1. Unzip the downloaded file named com_virtuemart.2.0.18a_extract_first. targz.zip. This reveals two more files.

2. Log in to your Joomla! admin control panel by going to www.yoursite.com/ administrator, navigate to **Extensions | Extension Manager** from the top menu and you will see the following screenshot:

3. We will use the first option labeled **Upload Package File**. Click on **Browse** and find the recently extracted VirtueMart file named com_virtuemart.2.0.xx.tar.gz.

[Make sure that you *do not* select the file ending with ... ext_aio. tar.gz as we are not ready for that one yet.]

4. When you have selected the correct file you can click on **Upload & Install**.

5. You should now see something like the following screenshot. Don't worry about the warning. We will come to that in the next recipe when we do some basic configurations:

6. If you get an error about the size of the upload or your browser just whirs around and never completes the task then do this: use FileZilla to upload the `com_virtuemart.2.0.xx.tar.gz` file to the TMP folder in the root of your Joomla! installation folder.

7. You can now use the section labeled **Install from directory** to get things done.

8. After uploading the file just add `/com_virtuemart.2.0.xx.tar.gz` to the end of the default file path and click on **Install**. All should now be good. Any time the Joomla! package installer fails to upload and install a package then you can do the same.

 Any time the file is too large for the Joomla! **Upload Package File** option, just transfer it with FileZilla to the TMP folder and install via the **Install from directory** option. For security reasons, delete the package file when you are done!

9. The core VirtueMart product is now installed, but before we conclude this recipe, let's add the **VirtueMart AIO** (**all in one**) extensions. This is all the virtually essential, predeterminable VirtueMart settings and modules, all of which are neatly lumped together in one installation.

10. From the same **Extension Manager: Install** page, click on **Browse**, select the `com_virtuemart.2.0.xxx_ext_aio.tar.gz` file, and click on **Upload & Install**.

11. You might have noticed the following message:

> **You may directly uninstall this component. Your plugins will remain**

That is because once you have used the component and it has done its work it is no longer necessary to leave it installed. We will deal with that when we do some basic VirtueMart configuration later in this chapter.

How it works...

The two files that we uploaded and installed constitute an entire e-commerce system. They contain everything that you need to handle such as the complex products and shipping options, attach to payment gateways, and managing your inventory.

There's more...

Now would be a good time, especially if this is your first VirtueMart installation, to go and check out some of the features, buttons, and menus. Don't worry about configuring anything, we will start all that in the next recipe. Also, you will probably keep getting that **Safe path empty...** warning. Again, we will deal with that soon. From the top menu navigate to **Components | VirtueMart**. The following is the screenshot of VirtueMart:

Familiarizing yourself with VirtueMart

We will have a very brief look at each major VirtueMart section. By the end of this exploratory recipe, any reader new to VirtueMart will have a good feel for where to get things done.

Getting ready

Log in to your Joomla! admin panel.

How to do it...

Let's get used to VirtueMart with a hands-on exploration:

1. As we have done before, from the Joomla! control panel navigate to **Components | VirtueMart**.

2. Click on the big **Products** button. You could also use the left-hand menu and click on **Products**, then **Products** again to arrive at the same place.

 We will be spending plenty of time here in the next chapter. It is where we can add, remove, configure, enable, and disable the actual products that we sell.

3. If you look on the main left-hand menu you will see that in the **Products** drop-down, as well as the actual **Products** link, where we are at the moment, there are a number of other product-related options such as:

   - **Product Categories**: This is where we create the structure of our catalogue

   - **Custom Fields**: This is where we can define detailed attributes that we can then apply to our products

   - **Inventory** link: This helps us to monitor the stock levels

   - **Taxes and Calculation Rules**: This is just about gets its own whole chapter (*Chapter 3, Shipping and Taxes*)

   - **Product Reviews**: This kind of speaks for itself

4. Have a click on each of the options on the VirtueMart screen to see what is there. We will go into more detail on each.

5. Click on the **Orders and Shoppers** drop-down menu. You will see the following options:

  ❑ **Orders**: This tops the list and it is potentially the most exciting link. When your store is running right, you will spend a lot of time here, managing the orders that your customers have made.

  ❑ **Revenue Report**: This allows you to sort your ordered data by a multitude of criteria and the date ranges in order to see your sales, refunds (gasp!), and so on.

  ❑ **Shoppers**: This lets you view and edit the details of all your customers.

  ❑ **Shopper Groups**: This lets you create different types of customer, if perhaps you want to distinguish between wholesale and retail.

  ❑ **Coupons**: This allows you to create exciting discounts and coupon offers.

Following are the next set of buttons:

▶ **Manufacturers**: This helps you in managing and arranging the manufacturer, if the manufacturer is an important distinction in your catalog.

▶ **Shop**: In this menu we will do the fundamental configuration, starting in the next recipe.

▶ **Shipping and Payments**: This option will teach us how to devise simple yet appropriate options for our customers, to have their orders sent, and to pay you.

▶ **Configuration**: This menu is deep and wide. We will be popping in here throughout many of the chapters. Notice how some of the options have long sprawling pages and multiple tabs as well (yuck!). I promise it is not as bad as it looks and we will break it down into the individual recipes as we proceed.

▶ **Tools**: This menu consists of a number of links to different help sources including the VirtueMart forum.

▶ **Tools and Migration**: This section consists of a few kinds of **Self Destruct** buttons, so it is a good place to play VirtueMart Russian roulette, but we will look at how and when to use them properly too. It is probably best not to click on them yet.

How it works...

By dividing up all the functions of VirtueMart into logical (fairly logical anyway) areas, it keeps the control panel from having overly complicated forms and buttons. If it looks complex then it is only because it is unfamiliar. Soon you will be clicking and configuring without a care.

Removing the VirtueMart AIO component

Remember the warning we received about removing the AIO component in the *Installing Joomla! 2.5 in your web space* recipe? We can delete the AIO component because its only purpose in life was to install some VirtueMart settings. Now it has been done, so we will remove it.

Getting ready

We are just going to whiz through this so we can get onto the next thing. So log in to your Joomla! control panel and we will get it done!

How to do it...

Let's remove the AIO component using the following steps:

1. Navigate to **Extensions | Extension Manager** and then click on the **Manage** tab.
2. You can find the required entry quickly by typing `allinone` into the **Filter** box and clicking on **Search**.
3. Select the **VirtueMart_allinone** checkbox. The following is a screenshot showing all of these steps together:

4. Now click on the **Uninstall** icon and then we can move on, burdened with a little bit less baggage than before.

How it works...

Very simply we have removed a component as a matter of good e-commerce housekeeping, sort of like "taking out the trash".

Creating a link to our store

The next minor issue is of being able to visit your store from the front end. If you go then you will find that the front end (customer facing) part of your store isn't there! We will fix this with a main menu link.

Getting ready

Log in to the Joomla! control panel if you are not there already.

How to do it...

To create the link to your store we will use the features of Joomla!:

1. Navigate to **Menu | Main Menu | Add New Menu Item**. We now have this on the left-hand side of the new **Menu Item** screen. Look at the following screenshot:

2. Click on the **Select** button next to the first option **Menu Item Type**. From the list under the **VirtueMart** heading choose **Front Page**.

3. For **Menu Title**, enter the word or words that will appear in the main menu. I chose `Shop`. That will do. We will revisit other settings when we look at topics such as SEO and templates in later chapters.

4. Click on **Save** on the top right of the screen.

How it works...

VirtueMart is installed and working but we needed to create a way to visit it. This simple link to the `Shop` home page is the first of a number of different ways of accessing your new store.

Removing the currency not defined error

At this point, it is likely that you will have these unsightly errors on the home page. Let's get rid of the **COM_VIRTUEMART_CONF_WARN_NO_CURRENCEY_DEFINED** error. The error will be displayed as shown in the following screenshot:

How to do it...

Removing this error will only take a minute:

1. In your admin panel navigate to **Components | VirtueMart**.

2. Now from the menu on the left, click on **Shop** and choose the SHOP link that is immediately below it. In the top left is the following form in the **Vendor Information** box.

3. Just enter a name for your business and a name for your shop. Then click on **Save**.

4. Click on **Configuration**, then click on **Currencies**, unpublish everything, then select the currencies you want, and then continue. Now on the right-hand side you will see the **Currency** box as shown in the following screenshot:

5. Go ahead and select your currency in the top box. In the box below that, you can click on it to accept another currency. Do this for every currency you want to accept. Now click on the **Save** button in the top right of the screen and the currency warning will disappear.

How it works...

VirtueMart now knows which currencies to use and has removed the unsightly error.

There's more...

When you click on the **Save** button, the currency warning will disappear but another message prompt will magically appear as shown in the following screenshot:

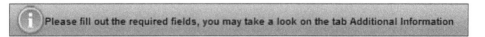

Filling out the company information section

We will get rid of this new distraction now.

How to do it...

Fill in the details as follows:

1. As suggested in the message, click on the **Additional Information** tab just below the message itself.

2. Scroll to the bottom of the page and you will see the following form as shown in the screenshot but without any data in it:

 Clearly, no explanation of what to fill in the form is necessary, just to say that what you enter is what your store will show to the public. So, if you are entering a phone number or other pertinent information, make sure it is the business information that you want the world to know about.

3. And don't forget to click on **Save** in the top right-hand corner when you are done.

How it works...

VirtueMart was just warning us that the most basic information required to configure the store was missing. Now it is entered, the warning is gone. We will enter more data about your company soon.

See also

▸ The *Fixing the safe path warning* recipe

Fixing the safe path warning

We are making rapid progress. Remember the **Safe path empty...** warning? Here we will fix it.

Getting ready

Log in to Joomla! and go to the **VirtueMart control panel**.

How to do it...

This will only take a minute:

1. Click on the drop-down menu titled **Configuration**. Immediately below is a **Configuration** link, click on that too. The following screenshot shows the warning that appears at the top of the page:

> Warning, the Safe Path is empty, for safety reasons it is very important to create a folder in a path not accessible by an URL, create also a folder Invoices in it to store your sensitive data secure. Our suggested path is for your system /home   /public_html/vmfiles, use this link to the config

2. The safe path warning requires us to make a folder outside of the publicly accessible web folder, where VirtueMart can store sensitive data (credit card info, text messages from previous partners, and so on).

 We are going to do what it says on the warning but we will choose our own folder name for a bit of added security. No website can be made hacker proof. But if we move sensitive data to an area of your web space that cannot be accessed directly or via a simple URL, then we force a would-be hacker to work harder to get that data. Once these steps are complete VirtueMart will use the new folders.

3. Create a new folder in the location suggested. It should be the folder up from the working Joomla! install. So the new folder will be in the same folder as the Joomla! install folder but not in the Joomla! install folder itself.

4. Name the folder something memorable but not obvious such as vm_stuff. Not too intriguing but clear to you.

5. Inside the vm_stuff folder create another folder and call it invoices.

6. Now we will tell VirtueMart where it is and what we called it. The actual path to this folder will vary depending upon your web host and your specific situation. So this is a consistent way to describe how to get your path accurately.

7. In your Joomla! control panel click on **Site | Global Configuration** and select the **System** tab. You will see a box labeled **Path to Log Folder**. The following screenshot shows the path that we need:

8. On the end of the path is your `joomlafolder/logs`. Copy the path excluding your `joomlafolder/logs`. Make sure to leave the trailing / on in the end. Now, we will paste it into the appropriate place in VirtueMart and add the `vm_stuff` at the end.

9. Navigate to **Components | VirtueMart**, then from the left-hand menu, select the **Configuration** and choose the **Templates** tab. Scroll near the bottom of the screen until you see the following screenshot:

Safe Path

10. Paste the path you copied earlier and add the name of the folder you created onto the end of the trailing /. Click on **Save**. The warning will be gone.

How it works...

By defining the safe path, VirtueMart can now put certain information a little bit further out of harm's way.

Setting up your company identity in VirtueMart

You might remember in a previous recipe we had entered some basic personal information such as name and address. We did this because VirtueMart wouldn't let us save/change anything else until we did it. Now we have tidied up all those niggling warnings, we can revisit and enter full details for our new store to be, as well as taking care of some of the e-commerce must-haves at the same time.

Getting ready

Now we can blast through this recipe as quickly as possible. The following are a few things to have in hand:

- A really cool logo for your store/company. A bit more on acquiring this is in the chapter on design and layout.

- A copy of your store's terms of service. There are lots of free terms of service templates on the web but this is one of those few areas where it might be worth spending a few dollars on advice, specific to your company, especially if you are selling something unusual, bespoke or controversial.

- Have to hand any further legal information.

- Here is the important one—a really neat description of your business and who you are. A kind of About us but more interesting than all those dull About us pages out there. You can use images in this description as well.

How to do it...

Here's how you can set up your company's identity in a few simple steps:

1. Go to your VirtueMart control panel. Click on **Shop**, either from the left-hand menu or the big icon in the main part of the page as shown in the following screenshot:

2. Scroll down to the following screenshot:

3. Browse to your pre-prepared logo and upload it. Now we could finish the recipe first but it is always a good idea to save changes as you go. If you get a phone call and leave the control panel, then after a short period of time, you will be logged out and your changes will be lost.

4. So click on **Save** in the top right of the screen.

5. Scroll down and in the **Description box** paste your neat description. Click on **Save**. Repeat these simple steps for your terms of service and legal information.

How it works...

VirtueMart has just created three pages based on the information you just entered. Now if you visit your shop front then you will notice they are not there yet. What we need to do is make them available to your customers through some links. That will be the topic of the next recipe.

Creating a menu for your must-have information

So where is all the information that we have entered into VirtueMart so far? It is tucked away in the VirtueMart database waiting for someone to summon it. The way that we achieve this is by linking to it.

Getting ready

Log in to your Joomla! control panel if you are not there already.

How to do it...

We will create a menu of links to the page that we created in the previous recipe. Then we will create a Joomla! module. A module is a deployable container. We will then be able to assign our menu to the module and deploy it somewhere useful for our customers to use.

Creating the menu

1. In your Joomla! control panel navigate to **Menus | Menu Manager | Add New Menu**. You will see the following screenshot:

2. In the **Title** box enter the title that you want to appear for this menu, such as Our Shop or something similar.

3. In the **Menu type** box just make it the same as the **Title** but all lower case and replace spaces with underscores. So mine would be our_shop.

4. In the **Description** field I put all the must-have links. All of the examples I give should have the marks removed. Click on **Save & Close** in the top right of the screen.

5. Now hover over the **Menus** drop-down and then hover over the newly created menu. In my case that's Our Shop and click on **Add New Menu Item**. This might look like a somewhat complicated page but for now there is very little to it. We will revisit much of what we skip over when we look at the chapters on SEO and also design. The following screenshot depicts the important part of what you will see.

This is what we need to do for now.

6. Click on the **Select** button to the right of the **Menu Item Type** label. Scroll down to near the bottom of the pop up window and choose **Displays vendor details**.

7. The next box down, **Menu Title**, refers to the actual text that will make up the menu item (link) so put something like About Us. Click on **Save & Close**. It should be simple now to add as many standard VirtueMart links as you like to this menu. Why not go ahead and add a link to your terms of service?

8. Click on the **New** button near the top-right of the screen to get the **New Menu Item** configuration screen.

Creating the container module

This is made nice and simple for us by the Joomla! system. Click on **Menus** and you should see a list of menus. In my list there are just two. One main menu and the other is the menu we just created. Look over to the right of the menu we just created and there is a helpful hint on what to do next, as shown in the following screenshot:

1. Click on the **Add a module for this menu type** link shown in the previous screenshot. The Joomla! system has kindly created a ready-to-configure module for us. All we need to do is fill in the blanks.

2. We could have got to the same place manually by navigating to **Extensions | Module Manager | New**. Also, note on the right-hand side that our menu has already been assigned to this module, as shown in the following screenshot:

3. We would have had to do these ourselves if we had decided to go the manual route. So let's finish off this module and display it to the world. Choose a title for our new module and click on the button to choose if you want the title to be shown on your site.

4. Try both ways if you are not sure what the difference will be. The following screenshot shows you exactly where to do this:

5. Finally, we need to decide where to show the module on the site. Click on the **Select position** button and choose where to display the module. If you are new to Joomla! this is a really good time to experiment.

6. Choose the **position-7** position which is top-left.

7. Click on **Save** and have a look at your site to view the changes, as shown in the following screenshot:

How it works...

VirtueMart is a component of Joomla!. Therefore it is often necessary to interact with Joomla! itself in order to achieve things in VirtueMart. Just then, we basically made a Joomla! menu using predefined (by the VirtueMart component) VirtueMart links, then placed that menu in a Joomla! module, and displayed it to the world.

There's more...

If you are new to Joomla! and all these modules, menus, and positioning them are getting you down, then the next recipe might help. We will be enabling and positioning some of the everyday VirtueMart modules such as the shopping cart. This should help you begin to understand the relationship between the different aspects of Joomla! and its components. We will do this in the next recipe.

Even if this apparent complexity does not evaporate entirely, it is enough to know at this stage that the complexity is for good reasons. It provides us with the properties of flexibility and extendibility. When you finally get your head round Joomla!, you will realize you can do almost anything with it.

Also every recipe in this book, although they do get more in depth, will show every click along the way. So a complete understanding will not be necessary to get things done.

Displaying the core VirtueMart menus

Now we will display and arrange some of the VirtueMart modules. Let's try and do this in a way that might be used in our final trading Joomla! e-commerce site. Of course, you probably have very specific layout plans. But this recipe should show enough of the ins and outs for you to make any modifications to suit your plan.

Getting ready

First we need a plan. Here is a good one. We want a product search in the top right and a product category box on the left of the module. Next we want a shopping cart on the right with a currency choice selector under that. Basic, but functional.

How to do it...

Let's start with the product search box. This is distinct from the regular Joomla! search box that searches the Joomla! articles. You might have noticed that the VirtueMart search box is already enabled for us. So we just need to move it to the top right of our site:

1. Navigate to **Extensions** | **Module Manager**. Near the top of the list you will see the **VM-Search in Shop** module.

2. Notice in the **Position** column it is shown as in **position-4**. This is what we need to change, as shown in the following screenshot:

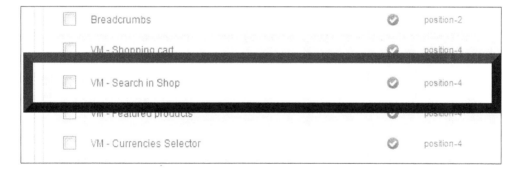

3. Click on **VM - Search in Shop**. You now see the following screenshot:

4. Click on the **Select Position** button and choose **position-0**. This does assume you haven't changed the template from the default one. If you have, it doesn't matter, just look down the **Templates** column for the search position for your template.

5. Click on **Save** when you are done. Check the store front and you should see your product search box neatly positioned.

   Next we will position the Product Categories box. Now at the moment we don't have any product categories but we will in the next chapter. So let's position it on the left ready.

6. If you are not on the **Module Manager** screen, then navigate to **Extensions | Module Manager** from the main Joomla! menu.

7. Now click on the **New** button. You will see the **Select a module** type pop up. Click on **VirtueMart Category** and you will then be able to fine-tune the module.

8. Let's name ours `Categories`. Click on the **Select Position** button and choose **position-4**. In the following screenshot it shows what the key parts of the configuration will look like when you are done:

9. **position-4** is the same position that the **VM - Search in Shop** module was in before we moved it. Click on **Save** to position your new module. You can't see it yet. But it is there.

Now we want the shopping cart and the **Currency Selection** box on the right. Notice they are already visible but on the left. The following steps show how to move them over:

1. Go to the **Module Manager** page (you know where it is).
2. First click on **VM - Shopping Cart**.
3. Click on the **Select Position** button and change the position to `position-8`.
4. Click on **Save**. Done! Now do the same for the **Currency Selector** box.

How it works...

Page layout in Joomla! is done with modules. Modules can be custom-made like the **Menu** module we created previously or can be predefined but with optional settings like the modules we just positioned.

There's more...

Did you notice that in the main **Module Manager** page there were a few more modules than those which actually exist on the site pages? Remember the **Product Categories** module that was seemingly invisible? Well, there are a number of other VirtueMart modules which are already enabled for us that will seemingly spring to life when there is some relevant content to show in them. We will get to that in the next chapter when we look at merchandising your VirtueMart store.

2
Merchandising VirtueMart

In this chapter we will cover:

- ▸ Adding manufacturers and manufacturer categories
- ▸ Implementing your product category structure
- ▸ Adding a simple product (information tab)
- ▸ Adding a simple product (description tab)
- ▸ Adding a simple product (status tab)
- ▸ Adding a simple product (dimensions and weight tab)
- ▸ Adding a simple product (images tab)
- ▸ Adding similar products
- ▸ Custom fields – adding consistent global information to multiple products
- ▸ Custom fields – customizing products with versions and charging different prices for them
- ▸ Custom fields – show related products on the product details page
- ▸ Custom fields – adding customizable product text and charging per letter
- ▸ Custom fields – creating groups of custom fields
- ▸ Setting the product and category, sort, and search options

Introduction

This chapter is packed full of recipes to help you get your VirtueMart store stocked up. The recipe titles speak for themselves and should make it obvious which recipes are for you. What is not so clear, however, is the extent to which you might need to do some planning before diving into a recipe. This is especially true if you are building your store from scratch.

Successful merchandising

In successful merchandising we look at writing your product descriptions. Not rocket science, although there is an art to writing product descriptions that sell. While that art form is too wide a subject to cover properly in this book, we will look at writing effective sales copy in *Chapter 6, Killer SEO*.

What is also regularly overlooked or at least put off until later, is the aspect of **Search engine optimization** (**SEO**). SEO to a large extent takes place after the website is launched. But the most basic and fundamental building block of any SEO campaign should ideally be dealt with before a single line of sales copy is written.

What is your keyword strategy? What are the words you will target in your forthcoming SEO campaign? You need to know that before you write your category and product descriptions, because you need to use those words in your product and category descriptions. Therefore it is worthwhile considering at least dipping into some of the recipes in *Chapter 6, Killer SEO* before this chapter.

Furthermore, with regards to SEO, in this chapter we will constantly be coming across opportunities to enter our metadata and search engine friendly (SEF) URLs. That is our keyword lists, page titles, and most importantly, meta descriptions. If you have already planned your keyword strategy and understand exactly how to write and implement this metadata, you can enter it all as you proceed through the various recipes in this chapter, saving time coming back to it later.

As just implied any discussion of keyword strategies, copy writing and metadata, and so on would be out of place in this chapter, but if any of the subjects are alien or unclear, you would save time and write better sales copy by looking at parts of *Chapter 6, Killer SEO* first.

Just do whatever works best for you.

Adding manufacturers and manufacturer categories

So you have decided that having the option of organizing your products by manufacturer is right for your business. This really quick and simple recipe will show you how.

You just need to decide if you are going to configure only manufacturers or manufacturers and categories. If your store only uses a few manufacturers or even a fairly large range of manufacturers then you probably don't need to define or separate them into categories.

Manufacturer categories are completely distinct from product categories although they work to organize your product range in a similar way.

If your manufacturers come from a diverse range of product types or are quite numerous, then manufacturer categories are almost certainly a good idea. You can organize the categories in almost any way you like. The trick to ensuring effective organization is to think about how they could be most useful to your customers.

Here are a few typical scenarios to help you think about the best strategy for your store.

The following is an example of a flat manufacturer's structure.

If you are selling laptops and nothing but laptops there is probably a really good case for a flat manufacturer structure. There are likely not dozens of laptop manufacturers in a typical laptop store and, in this context, all do the exact same thing, manufacture laptops. So no manufacturer categories would probably be appropriate.

The following is an example of a typical structure using categories.

Assume that you expand your laptop shop to sell laptop bags and consumables. The number of manufacturers will obviously grow and their nature becomes more diverse. Shoppers might like to browse by manufacturer, but if they are looking for laptop bags, they might not be able to easily distinguish between laptop bags, consumables or laptop manufacturers. Creating categories of manufacturers, consumables, laptops, and bags will certainly make their browsing more pleasing and, therefore, make a purchase more likely.

The following is an example of a vast manufacturer structure.

Now imagine you open a wholesale site and you expand to sell everything computing from screen wipes, through components, to custom built server systems. All of a sudden the situation has changed in two ways. First, you now have a manufacturer base numbering at least in the hundreds,
 and second, your typical shopper has changed. A wholesale purchaser might be very familiar with who manufactures what. Now it might be best to organize your manufacturer categories alphabetically.

Getting ready

Think and plan for the best category structure for helping your customers. If you want to have images or logos on your manufacturer pages, then have them to hand before you move on. Likewise have any descriptions or manufacturer contact details that you might want to use. These can be in a plain text format such as Windows Notepad because VirtueMart has an HTML editor for adding structure or it can be in already formatted HTML so that you can paste directly into the editor.

How to do it...

If you have decided you do not need manufacturer categories, skip ahead to adding manufacturers. To add manufacturer categories, follow these steps:

1. In the VirtueMart control panel click on the **Manufacturers** menu and then the **Manufacturer categories** link.

2. Now click on the **New** button in the top right of the **Manufacturer categories** area. The page looks like the following screenshot:

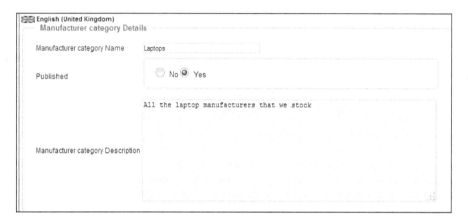

3. Now add the category title and a brief description of what manufacturers the category will contain.

4. Click on the **Save and Close** button. Now repeat the preceding process for all your categories. Here is what our **Manufacturer categories** page looks like after we have implemented the simple category structure example described earlier:

Adding manufacturers:

1. In the VirtueMart control panel click on the **Manufacturers** link.
2. Now click on the **New** button. Notice on this screen you have two tabs. One is for the majority of what we need to fill in, the **Description** tab, and the other is for uploading images, if you wish to, the **Image** tab. The following screenshot is of the **Description** tab:

3. Enter the manufacturer's name in the first box. Leave the **Published** option checked to **Yes**. The **Manufacturer SEF Alias** field will be covered fully in *Chapter 6, Killer SEO,* but if you are confident about defining a search friendly URL now, then go ahead.

4. If you have chosen to define manufacturer categories, go ahead and choose the appropriate category in the **Manufacturer category Name** drop-down box. Otherwise skip this step.

The next two options shown in the following screenshot are worth considering a little:

As the labels make clear, this is where you can put a link to the manufacturer's website and a contact e-mail address. If you have a special relationship with a niche manufacturer, then you might be confident adding the details. If so, add them now. More likely you might want to skip these two options because sending your customer off to some faceless big corporation's website might well be the last you see of them. Equally, unless you have special reason to do so, you probably want them to e-mail you with queries, not the manufacturer. Moving on:

1. Paste your pre-prepared manufacturer's description into the **Description** box. Click on the **Images** tab.

2. At first sight this might look like a fairly complex page. Most of the options are for future management of your images and selecting pre-uploaded images. All we need to do now is scroll to the bottom of the page until we see the following box in the screenshot:

3. Just click on **Browse...**, find the appropriate manufacturer image and upload it. Now click on **Save** and you can fill out the last couple of fields.

If you accidentally clicked on **Save and Close** instead of **Save**, just open up the manufacturer you were working on by selecting it from the list.

The last optional bits of information are to add a subtitle to your image or image alt text for visitors to your site who browse on text-or speech-based browsers. Adding this is also useful for search engines identifying the nature of your image. The following screenshot is what you're looking for:

4. Click on **Save and Close**. Repeat the preceding steps until you have entered all your manufacturers.

For displaying your manufacturers to your customers, use the following steps. If you followed the setup recipes in *Chapter 1, Setting Up Shop,* then you already have a **Manufacturers category** box in the bottom left of your store front:

1. Click on the **Manufacturers category** box to expand it and then choose a manufacturer or manufacturer category.

2. If you need to display the manufacturer category box, here is how to do it. From the Joomla! top menu choose **Extensions | Module Manager**. Now click on **New** and choose **VirtueMart Manufacturers** from the pop-up menu. The page looks like the following screenshot:

3. Just enter a title for your new module in the field labeled **Title** and choose a position by clicking on **Select Position**. Selecting **position-4** will put your new manufacturer categories module in the bottom left of your site. The page looks like the following screenshot:

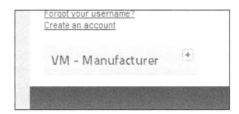

How it works...

All the data that we entered for manufacturers and categories goes into the VirtueMart database. This then enables us to use the almost pre-configured VirtueMart manufacturers category module, to allow our customers to browse our manufacturers.

There's more...

We did skip over some minor details like SEF URLS, but these are best decided upon as part of a whole keyword strategy and that is covered in depth in *Chapter 6, Killer SEO*.

Implementing your product category structure

Implementing your product categories is technically easy if you have taken the time to plan them first. Think for a while about the most useful structure for your customers; particularly what makes it easy for them to find what they want. This is a process that will probably involve looking at your competitors, thinking about logically dividing up your range, as well as a bit of creative thinking.

This recipe will implement a category structure with one level of subcategories but it would be very easy to adapt it to implement a more complex structure or a simpler one with just top-level categories.

Getting ready

Before you get started make sure you have your category structure clearly mapped out on paper or in a text file. Also have in hand some excellent sales copy to describe your categories ready to paste into the appropriate places. VirtueMart can also accommodate category images and although these are optional they will likely enhance the appearance of your store if used.

How to do it...

Here we will create the first product category, then you can loop back until all the product categories you need are implemented. So let's do it:

1. In the VirtueMart control panel click on the **Products** menu and then **Product Categories**. Now click on the **New** button.

    First of all let's create all of our top level categories. If you don't have any subcategories then this is the only section you need to read.

    The first step is to fill out the fields in the **General Information** box at the top of the page. The page looks like the following screenshot:

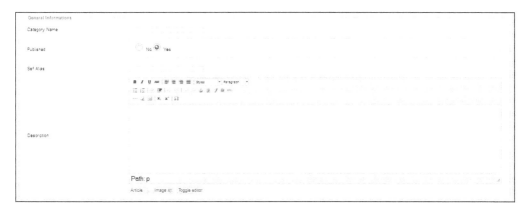

2. Enter the category name in the **Category Name** box. Leave the **Yes** button as it is for the **Published** label. With the **Sef Alias** option it is suggested deferring a choice until you have read *Chapter 6, Killer SEO*, but if you do know what you want your search friendly URL to be, then enter it here.

3. Finally for the **General Information** section paste your pre-prepared category descriptions into the **Description** box. Notice the buttons underneath:

    ❏ **Article**: Click on it to include an already published Joomla! article as your category description

    ❏ **Image**: Click on it to add an image to your description

    ❏ **Toggle editor**: By using this we can switch between raw HTML and the more friendly editor view. Use the raw HTML view for pasting raw HTML, and the editor view for formatting and tweaking your description

Now we will look at the **Details** box directly following where we have been working. Not quite as self-explanatory, but not complicated either. Many of the options are to do with the layout of your categories. We will look at this in much more detail in *Chapter 4, Making Your Store Look Amazing*. For some of the options to be useful we need to have installed a template. For now just look at the following two options:

The **Ordering** dropdown will allow you to set the position of the category you are creating.

As mentioned in the chapter introduction the **Meta Information** section is covered in *Chapter 6, Killer SEO*.

We are nearly there with our top-level categories. Click on the **Image** tab at the top of the page. All you need to do is scroll down to the **Browse...** button, click on it and select your pre-prepared category image. The page looks like the following screenshot:

Remember to click on **Save and Close**. Repeat the preceding steps until you have all your top level categories implemented.

You can also upload more than one image per category!

Implementing sub categories is so quick, it is almost funny. Do exactly as you did for the top-level categories. Click on **New**, fill out all the details, upload the image, and so on. But this time, when you are in the details section, find the following box:

Click on the **Category Ordering** dropdown and select the top-level category you would like this new category to be a sub category of. That was a bit of a mouthful. Look at the following screenshot. There you can see a 7 inch tablet sub category in the **Tablets** top-level category. The page looks like the following screenshot:

And in the following screenshot you can see how this is represented on the Categories main page:

Repeat for all your sub categories and if you have any sub categories of sub categories, simply select the sub category instead of a top-level category in the preceding step.

Adding a simple product (information tab)

The information tab is the first one we come to when adding a new product in VirtueMart. We will be using an example of a range of e-commerce movies and related products to demonstrate the different product features of VirtueMart. If you have already read any of the *Custom fields* recipes you will know why this is useful.

Getting ready

Log in to Joomla! admin and go to the VirtueMart control panel. Now select **Products | Products** from the left-hand menu and **New** from the top row of buttons.

How to do it...

First we will enter the basic product information. The page looks like the following screenshot:

1. Make sure that the **Published** checkbox is checked or the product won't appear.

2. Enter the EAN barcode or SKU, if you use them, in the **Product SKU** field. Now enter the actual product name that will appear to customers in the **Product Name** field. **Product Alias** can be left blank because VirtueMart will sort that out for us and leave the **URL** field blank too. The page looks like the following screenshot:

3. Click on the **Manufacturer** dropdown, if you have any manufacturers, and choose one from the list.

4. Click on the **Product Categories** dropdown and choose all the categories you want this to appear in. We have an **E-commerce movies** category and a **CMS Movies** category. As this product is **VirtueMart the Movie**, the appropriate category is chosen. That's it for this box, for now. As we are configuring a simple product, we don't need to concern ourselves with the details here. The page will look like the following screenshot:

5. Simply enter the all inclusive price in your main currency into the **Final price** field. Now check the **Calculate Cost Price** checkbox. We are almost done.

6. Scroll down until you see the **Internal note** form field, as shown in the following screenshot, and enter any information that might help you remember pertinent facts about this product.

> Internal note
>
> This DVD is a bit grainy so might get the occasional complaint.
> I must read chapter 3 of John's book to set up taxes and shopper groups.
> And if I am going to offer multiple versions of this movie I should
> read the Product Field recipes in this chapter!

7. Click on **Save**.

How it works...

We have entered the bare minimum required to have a live product in VirtueMart. The next recipes will build on that to have a much fuller offering.

There's more...

Go check out your first product in your store. It's quite basic and not likely to attract too many buyers, but we will build on it without further delay. The page looks like the following screenshot:

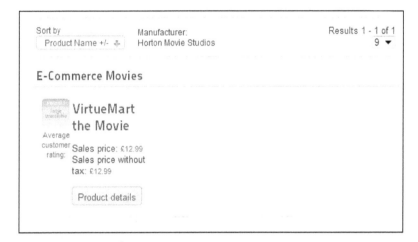

Adding a simple product (description tab)

Now we will look at the next tab along and make our product more enticing. A good description can make or break the sale. It should not just be the raw uninteresting details that we enter here but the enticing product selling points that prompt a customer to part with their money.

Getting ready

Have a think about how to describe your product in a highly enticing way using the keywords in your keyword strategy, if you have one. See *Chapter 6, Killer SEO* if you want help with this.

How to do it....

Add a simple product using the following steps:

1. If you are still in the product page just click on the **Product Description** tab. If not, navigate back to the VirtueMart products page and click on your product, then the **Product Description** tab.

2. Copy and paste from Notepad or type your enticing description into the **Product Description** field and an abridged version into the **Short Description** field, as shown in the following screenshot:

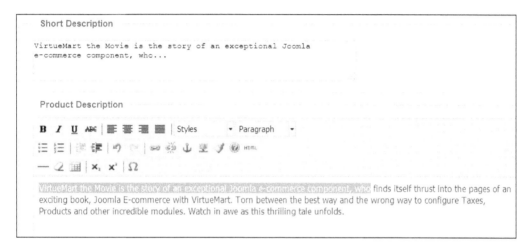

Near the bottom of the **Product Description** field you have the following buttons:

You can use them to include images in your product description as well as switch to the HTML view if you want to paste HTML or tweak the code by hand.

3. Click on **Save**. This is all we need to do for now.

How it works...

We have now added a cool description of our product to the VirtueMart database.
The full description will be shown on the actual product page and the short description
on the category page, as shown in the following screenshot:

See also

▶ The *Entering your metadata into VirtueMart* recipe in *Chapter 6, Killer SEO*.

Adding a simple product (status tab)

Status refers to things like stock levels, level warnings, and carton and selling quantities.

Getting ready

A mini stock take on the product you are configuring would be good preparation here.

How to do it...

Add a simple product using the **Status** tab:

1. Click on the **Product Status** tab and you will be faced with the following screenshot:

   OK, top to bottom left to right. This is what we have to do:

2. How many do you have in stock? Enter the quantity in the **In Stock** field. Do you want to be notified of having low or no stock? Enter the level to be alerted in the **Low Stock Notification** field.

   Want to enforce a minimum purchase quantity? This is useful when you have a price per unit but multiple units must be purchased together.

3. Enter the value in the **Minimum Purchase Quantity** box.

4. If the product is currently unavailable, enter the date they will be available by clicking on the **Availability Date** box and selecting the date from the handy calendar, as shown in the following screenshot:

The similarly titled but different in function **Availability** box is for entering an estimated time to arrival after purchase. You can enter something in the text field or choose one of the VirtueMart supplied graphics from the dropdown, as shown in the following screenshot:

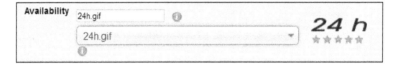

5. Next we will look at the next column of options: the first is **Booked, ordered products**. This is useful for stock control. You might have ten in stock, but if eleven are booked/ordered, then you don't want to sell any more unless the customer knows the availability situation. Enter any booked/ordered product quantities here.

6. **Purchase Quantity Steps** ties in with the **Minimum Purchase Quantity**. If your product comes in packs of six, then your **Purchase Quantity Steps** should be set to 6 as well as the **Minimum Purchase Quantity**.

7. Then the customer can purchase any quantity they like as long as it is a multiple of six. Here it is in action in the store, with both values set to 6, as shown in the following screenshot:

8. Every time the customer clicks on **+** or **-** the quantity increases/decreases by six.

9. Finally the **Maximum Purchase Quantity** will prevent the customer from selecting any quantity of products beyond that amount. Enter your maximum here, or leave blank to allow unlimited quantities to be purchased.

How it works...

Applying quantities to create simple rules for VirtueMart to follow helps make our lives administering our shop, once it is trading, a whole lot easier.

Adding a simple product (dimensions and weight tab)

This section is only necessary if you will be calculating your shipping based on dimensions or weight. Here is what to do.

Getting ready

You should have to hand all of the product weights and dimensions. Also have to hand the overall weight including any packaging it will be shipped in.

How to do it...

Adding a simple product using the **Product Dimensions and Weight** tab:

1. Click on the **Product Dimensions and Weight** tab. You will see the following self-explanatory screen:

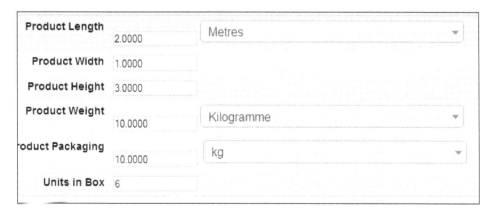

2. But filling it in accurately will make life a lot easier when we configure shipping by weight in *Chapter 3, Shipping and Taxes*.

3. Make sure to select the correct units of measurement for product dimensions (**M**, **CM**, **MM**, **Yards**), product weight (**Gramme**, **Kilogramme**, **Pounds**, **Ounces**), and product packaging weight(**Kilogramme**, **Metres**, **Metres squared**, **cubed** and so on).

4. For this option choose the unit of measurement that the shipping company works in. Then, lastly, indicate how many units go into each packaging item.

5. Click on **Save**.

How it works...

Initially there appears to be no effect from doing this. But the details are stored away in the VirtueMart database just waiting for some shipping options to be configured.

See also

▸ The *Configuring shipping by a combination of criteria* recipe in *Chapter 3, Shipping and Taxes*

▸ The *Charging for shipping by weight range* recipe in *Chapter 3, Shipping and Taxes*

Adding a simple product (images tab)

Now for the pretty stuff. Adding an image will really improve the presentation of your product.

Getting ready

Have to hand all your main product images and we will now go and add them to your catalog.

How to do it...

Make sure you are on the product you want to add images for and then we will get started.

1. Click on the **Product Images** tab. Scroll to the bottom of the page to find the following screenshot:

2. Click on **Browse...**, find and select your product image. Next click on the **Save** button from the row of buttons at the top of the page.

3. Take a look at how the image appears in your store. Have a look on the product page and the category page. The page will look like the following screenshot.

 You can upload more than one image per product. Just repeat the steps in the preceding recipe and VirtueMart will create a neat little gallery for you.

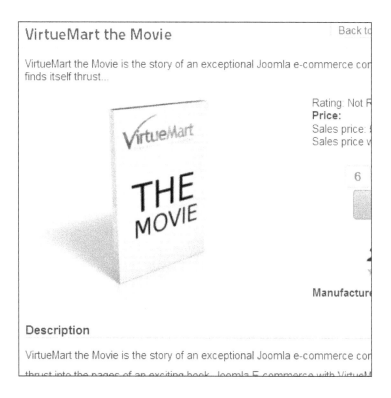

4. Now you can scroll back down to the area shown in the following screenshot and enter a title to be displayed with your image and some image alt text, to describe your image to customers on text-or speech-based browsers.

Displayed image subtitle	The DVD
Image Alt-Text	Picture of VirtueMart The Movie DVD

5. Remember to click on **Save**.

How it works...

Now we have added an image to the VirtueMart database. VirtueMart was able to not only save a copy for use on the product page, but it has also created a small version (thumbnail) to use in the category view, alongside the short description.

Adding similar products

This is so easy I almost left it out! However, the potential time saved using cloning is huge. So I thought of showing this to you, in case you haven't figured it out for yourself yet.

As we have discovered, creating a product with all the various tabs can be a long process. In VirtueMart we can clone a product into an identical, yet new product. We then have the opportunity to go into that product's settings and alter them. So we need to decide which (if any) of our product range would be quicker to amend an existing product than it would be to start from scratch.

Also note that you can clone a product, alter it, then clone the altered product. Careful planning here can save a lot of time, if you have lots of similar products in your catalog.

Getting ready

Make a cloning plan.

How to do it...

Cloning is a lot less painful than it sounds. Just three steps:

1. Go to the main products page by clicking on the **Products** link in the **Products** menu. Select the checkbox on the left of the product to be cloned as shown in the following screenshot:.

2. Click on the **Clone** button in the row of buttons at the top of the page as shown in the following screenshot:

3. Click on the cloned product and edit it according to the requirements. Fields that will probably need changing are **Product_alias** on the **Product Information** tab (VirtueMart just appends a number to this but they might not be what you want), the product name, and other essentials like weight, price, and so on. Repeat the preceding steps.

How it works...

VirtueMart very simply makes a duplicate product for you to edit. Helpfully it omits to copy attributes like stock level and price, which are likely to be different, but copies likely to be required information like other product status details.

There's more...

Also note that as you would logically expect, child products are not cloned automatically. So if you cloned a product with multiple versions implemented through a custom field for child products you will get an error on the product page as shown in the following screenshot:

> **Warning**: Invalid argument supplied for foreach() in **/home/bvdcdmru/public_html /joomla25/plugins/vmcustom/stockable/stockable.php** on line 229

To remove it, simply delete the custom field from the **Custom Field** tab of the cloned product. Don't forget to **Save** afterwards.

See also

▸ The *Custom fields – customizing products with versions and charging different prices for them* recipe

Custom fields – adding consistent global information to multiple products

Supposing there is a bit of information that is relevant to some or all of your products. Then consider that the information might change from time to time. Perhaps you have 100 products out of 150 that all come with a 30 day money back guarantee. You could enter that guarantee information into the product description. But what if you then change it to a 60 day guarantee? Even worse, what if some products changed to 60 days, some stayed the same, and some needed the guarantee removed?

Custom fields were designed for such nightmares. What we will do in this recipe is create a simple text custom field for 30 days money back guarantee.

Then you will be able to add or remove a custom field or edit the custom field using the information gained in this recipe and, as if by magic, all the products with that custom field will change too.

Getting ready

These simple text custom fields can be any text at all. Think about where you would need a consistent textual field in your store and read on to implement it.

How to do it...

First create the custom fields. Steps for creating the custom fields are as follows:

1. Click on the **Custom Fields** tab from the **Products** menu on the left and click on the **New** button from the row of buttons near the top. You will see the following page:

I admit it, this looks like a bit of an administrator's nightmare. But it is what gives VirtueMart a lot of its options and flexibility. With this one form you can create so many different features. That is why there are so many recipes on custom fields. Here is how to implement this one in 60 seconds or less:

2. In the **Custom Field Type:** dropdown select **String**. String means text.

3. In the **Title** field type, `30 day money back guarantee` or whatever your standard text needs to say.

4. Then in **Default** enter a description that relates to the title. This could be changed on a per product basis. Here `QUALIFIES` is entered for the guarantee.

5. Last of all you can enter a helpful tool tip in the **Tooltip** field. This is a pop-up message when the title is hovered over by the customer's mouse. The following is an abbreviated and concatenated screenshot of the form to show you what is entered:

6. Click on **Save**. Repeat for any other standard text you need to create.

Now let's add it to a product. Steps for adding the custom field to a product are as follows:

1. Select the product you want to add the custom field to from the main products page. You can get there by selecting **Products** from the **Products** menu.

2. Click on the **Custom Fields** tab, scroll to near the bottom, select the custom field you just made from the **Custom field type** dropdown. Click on **Save** and go and have a look at the text on your product in your store.

How it works...

You can now apply this custom field to any product that you like. It is true that future custom fields get a bit more complicated but a recipe at a time is a cinch.

There's more...

You could of course amend the text of your custom field, and all products assigned that custom field would also magically change.

Custom fields – customizing products with versions and charging different prices for them

Often you will have a product available in more than one version. What about a black or white iPad? Or the download, DVD or Blu-ray version of VirtueMart the Movie. Of course it would be easy to implement a new product for each version, but that is not always what you want. If it makes sense in your version dilemma to have the versions selectable on one product page, then this is the recipe for you. And VirtueMart will handle the stock control for each version separately.

Getting ready

Write down the different versions you will create and make a note of the products you intend to apply them to. Fire up VirtueMart and read on.

How to do it...

We will do this over two stages much like the other custom field recipes:

► First we create the custom field itself

► Then we will add the custom field to a product

Steps for creating the custom field are as follows:

1. In the **Products** menu click on the **Custom Fields** option. Now choose **New** from the row of buttons near the top.

2. In the **Custom Field type:** select **Plug-ins** as shown in the following screenshot:

3. Now in the **Title** field enter `Choose media type` or something similar that fits your goals. And in the **Cart Attribute** box be sure to select the **Yes** radio button.

4. When we selected the **Plug-ins** type we got an extra drop-down box to play with. In the **Select a plug-in** field choose **Stockable variants**. When you do a whole bunch of extra options there is a pop up, as shown in the following screenshot:

5. In **Option name** enter `Type` and on three separate lines enter `Download, DVD, Blu-ray`, or whatever your options will be. Click on **Save**.

Steps for adding the custom field to a product are as follows:

1. Now select **Products** from the **Products** menu and click on the product you want to add the custom field to. Click on the **Custom Fields** tab.

2. In the drop-down box in the **Custom field type** section choose your new custom field that we just made. The page will look like the following screenshot:

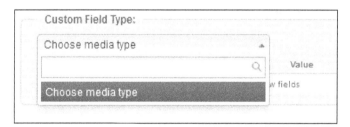

Now we see the following screenshot:

Please, add new child product! Thereafter you can select the option for each product
Parent
Variant   Type   Additional charge
    New Product

    Product SKU   Product Name   Additional charge

    Product in stock   ○ New

What is about to happen is that we will be configuring a child product. That is a product related to another product, in this case the VirtueMart the Movie product. VirtueMart will then magically add a child product for each option in our custom field and we will further configure each option/child as well. All from the preceding screenshot by using the following steps:

1. Enter the **Product SKU** for the first version of your product. Then enter a product name. The products used in this chapter are clearly homebrew, here it is,
   `VirtueMart the Movie - Download.`

2. Also enter a stock level. You can leave the other fields blank. Just click on the **New** button. Now look at what has happened. You can see we have the option to add another version as well as to further configure the initial one.

3. You can see that here -1 is typed for **Additional charge** and **Download** is selected in the **Type** dropdown. This means that the first option available to our customers will be the **Download** option and it will cost 1.0 of our native currency less than the main product, which is its parent, as shown in the following screenshot:

The following picture shows the area just following the preceding screenshot where you can create another version in the same way.

4. Enter the details for the next version and click on **New**. Configure the new version, perhaps like the one we have in the following screenshot.

5. I selected **DVD** for the **Type** dropdown and **0** for the **Additional charge**. This means the DVD version of the child product is the same price as the parent product. It looks like the following screenshot:

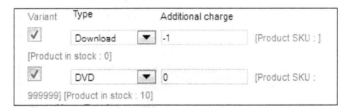

6. Just the Blu-ray left. So enter an SKU and a stock level as before, click on **New**, configure the version, and click on **Save**.

7. I added an extra 5 currency units to my Blu-ray version. This seems fair for such a high quality and high definition product.

8. Now click on **Save** and we will see what has happened.

How it works...

Select the **Products** link from the **Products** menu and we will see what has been going on behind the scenes.

You will see that VirtueMart has created three child products for us and that they are children to the VirtueMart the Movie product.

Now if we look at our shop front and go to the details page of the product we can see the product versions dropdown in action. Notice how the price changes when we select the different versions, as shown in the following screenshot:

There's more...

I found this process quite buggy. Not unreasonably so, but enough to make it slightly more challenging than it should have been.

 The custom fields section of VM has been completely rewritten for VM2.2, which will soon be available in the VM2.1 series of betas. So there may be changes to the recipe shown here.

On the **creating the custom field** section, when saving, if there are any fields the page doesn't like, it will clear all the fields. Make sure that all the options discussed are reselected, especially the **Cart Attribute** set to **Yes**. Failing to do this will make everything appear to be going according to plan when it isn't.

If things don't seem to work out for you on the 'adding the custom field to the product' part, try saving the page to give the JavaScript a kick-start.

If you get in a mess and find you have loads of child products and don't know what is going on (obviously this didn't happen to me), then delete the custom field (to remove it from the product) then delete the child products (See *Chapter 5, Going Live* for how to do this if you're, not sure). Now start a fresh.

Custom fields – show related products on the product details page

We can achieve so many things by using the custom fields tab of the product we want to show related products of. But this is simpler than other custom fields recipes, in that we don't have to create a custom field first. Showing related products is often a good idea as it encourages customers to make more purchases.

Getting ready

Make sure you have created the products you want to use as related products.

How to do it...

We have created Joomla! the Movie and we will be making it a related product to the VirtueMart the Movie product. Here is how to do it:

1. Select the **Products** links from the **Products** menu. Click on the product you want to add related products to. Now click on the **Custom Fields** tab of that product.

2. Scroll down to the **Related Products** search box and begin typing the name of the product you want this product to relate to, as shown in the following screenshot:

3. Click the product you want to add, click on **Save**, then search again and add any other products you want this one to relate to. Click on **Save**.

How it works...

If you go and visit the product details page, you will see that VirtueMart has created a custom field showing your related product(s), as shown in the following screenshot:

There's more...

You probably noticed while completing this recipe that you could use exactly the same process if you wanted the product to relate to a whole category of products. Just type your search and make your selections from the **Related Categories** section instead, as shown in the following screenshot:

Custom fields – adding customizable product text and charging per letter

Do you want to add custom or customer designed products to your store? What about a greeting in a card to make it personal or a player name on a football shirt? Here is how to do it with custom fields in VirtueMart.

Getting ready

Log in to Joomla! admin and select the VirtueMart component. The example used here is the option to add a custom message on the DVD when giving Joomla! the Movie to a close friend. Not only will they thank you for a life altering movie, but they will also feel like the gift is extra special because of the personal touch.

How to do it...

We will do this in two parts. First creating the custom field and then adding the field to a product.

Creating the custom field:

1. Select **Custom Fields** from the **Products** menu and then click on **New**. For **Custom Field Type** select **Plugins** as shown in the following screenshot:

2. For **Cart Attribute** choose **Yes** as shown in the following screenshot:

3. In the **Description** box type `Enter your personal message`. For **Plugin Type** choose **Customer Text Input** from the dropdown. You will now see the following screenshot:

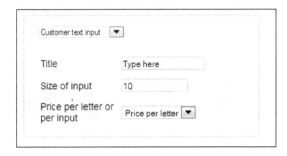

4. Now in the new fields that have opened up choose **Price per letter** from the dropdown and in the **Title** field delete what is in there by default and type **Type here**.

Adding the custom field to a product:

1. Click on the **Products** link in the **Products** menu and select the product you want to add the chargeable customizable text to.

2. Click straight on the **Product Fields** tab. Scroll down and from the dropdown selector choose **Type here** or whatever you called the custom field as shown in the following screenshot:

Nearly done. You can alter the maximum size of the message by entering a value in the **Size of input** field. The only thing you must do is enter a number for the cost per letter. In our example you can see we entered **1.0** which will be 1 of whatever your default currency. If your product is not as prestigious as mine you might like to reduce the cost per letter slightly.

3. Click on **Save** and look at the product details page in your shop.

How it works...

Notice that as you type into the message box, the product price automatically increases. And whatever the final price is, when you click on **Add to cart**, that is what is added.
If you ordered the product the message will be part of the invoice and product description, enabling us to make sure we prepare the product correctly before shipping, as shown in the following screenshot:

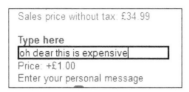

Custom fields – creating groups of custom fields

Now just suppose you want more than one custom field type on a whole range of products. You guessed it, you need to create a group or a parent. The existing custom fields can then be made into children of the parent. Clearly this is a slightly different order from how human parents get their children. We could think of the existing custom fields as orphans and the parent we will soon create as an adoptive parent. Yes that works better.

Getting ready

Choose the custom fields you are going to have adopted, by your soon to be created parent.

How to do it...

We are going to group together a couple of the custom fields from earlier recipes and add them to the Joomla! the Movie product:

1. Select the **Products** menu and then the **Custom Fields** link. Click on the **New** link and configure just the **Title** and the **Type** fields.

2. **Title** can be whatever will remind you what it is and **Type** must be **Parent**. See the following screenshot for clarification:

3. **Save** your new parent custom field, and from the list of your custom fields, click the first custom field you want to make a child of the parent. This is nice and easy.

4. Click the **Parent** dropdown and choose your newly created parent. Click on **Save**. It is now adopted. Repeat this last step for any others that you want to become a child of the parent.

Adding the parent custom field to a product:

1. Select the product to add the parent custom field to from the list of your products. Click on the **Custom Fields** tab.

2. Scroll down and select your parent custom field from the dropdown as shown in the following screenshot:

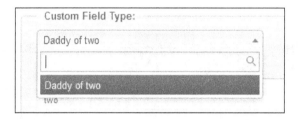

The following screenshot displays what you will see:

Configure the child custom fields the same way you did when they were not children and were presented on their own and click on **Save**.

How it works...

By combining multiple custom fields, by adding them to a parent to create a group, we can have lots of useful groups to suit all the product types in our catalog.

For exactly how to create and then configure the two children of the parent that have been added, please see the previous recipes.

See also

- ▸ The *Custom fields – adding customizable product text and charging per letter* recipe
- ▸ The *Custom fields – customizing products with versions and charging different prices for them* recipe

Setting the sort and search options for products and categories

This short recipe will conclude this chapter by setting how we want our products and categories to be seen, sorted, and searched. Exactly which settings you use will depend upon the goals of your store.

Getting ready

This recipe is divided into three short sections. Product and category sort order, which at the click of a drop-down list, will choose the order in which your shop's wares appear on the page. There are a surprising number of options.

Then we can choose from the same range of sort options and decide which of those options our customers should be allowed to choose from, if they want to change our default sort order.

And finally, we will take a look at choosing the fields we want our customers to be able to search for.

How to do it...

All of the preceding sections takes place on one handy page:

1. From the VirtueMart control panel open the **Configuration** menu, click on the **Configuration** option, and then the **Product Order Settings** tab.

The first two options we are faced with are the following:

The first dropdown chooses the order the products will appear in and the second your categories. How you do it depends on the objectives of your store.

Choose the best default sort order for your products and categories from their respective drop-down lists and click on **Save**.

Configuring the customer's sort options: the customer might not agree with your choice of sort order and could find it useful to be able to sort by their own preferred criteria. On the category pages that list products, the customer will see the following:

Every option that you put a check mark in from the available sort-by fields section will appear in the preceding drop-down list. The trick is not to check so many fields that the customer will be baffled, but to make sure the most useful options for your specific catalog are checked:

1. Click to bring up a check mark in anything useful, uncheck everything else, and click on the **Save** button.

2. Finally, let's look at the **Available search fields** section. This works a little differently to the last option, because what you configure makes no difference to the customer's user interface. But when they click into the search box and type their search term, what are they likely to be searching for in your store? Brands, sizes, model numbers, SKUs, or simple descriptions?

3. You need to consider your specific customers and your catalog and check everything useful, but only everything useful. Click on **Save** and we're done.

How it works...

By fine tuning areas like sorting and searching you make your customer's life easier. Anything you can do to make your customer click on the **Add to cart** button, and make it through your checkout, makes your store more profitable. The difference between a modestly successful store and a very successful store is not usually one big thing, but more often lots of little things. In *Chapter 5, Going Live* we will look at lots of the little things.

3
Shipping and Taxes

In this chapter we will cover the following:

- ► Charging for shipping by weight range
- ► Configuring shipping by country, zone, or continent
- ► Configuring shipping by zip code
- ► Configuring shipping by a combination of criteria
- ► Configuring VAT on the entire purchase (including or excluding VAT on delivery costs)
- ► Configuring a tax to start or finish on a set date
- ► Configuring a tax on a per-category basis

Introduction

Shipping and taxes in e-commerce might be one of the least entertaining topics to read about. But with a little bit of planning, the setup and configuration of the perfect tax and shipping rules for you can be made fairly trivial.

Shipping

The first three shipping recipes cover common scenarios and the fourth one covers how to combine multiple scenarios. The key to make each recipe really simple is a little bit of planning, which is discussed at the start of each recipe.

Taxes

Taxes as we will see are quite straightforward to implement in VirtueMart. However, understanding exactly which taxes at which rates you should implement is anything but straightforward. They of course vary from country to country, state to state, and zone to zone. Punishments for getting it wrong range from a small fine to imprisonment. If there is one area of e-commerce worth paying for advice, it is taxes. Consult an accountant/tax lawyer, implement their recommendations, and then get them to check and review those implementations on a regular basis.

On with the recipes now!!

Charging for shipping by weight range

This is the simplest shipping method of all, so we will jump in and configure it in a flash.

Getting ready

The only preparation you will need to have done is to assign weights to your products so that VirtueMart database knows how heavy everything is and can use the rules we create in a moment to calculate and charge the appropriate shipping cost.

If you haven't done that already, see the previous chapter and the *Adding a simple product (dimensions and weight tab)* recipe.

Now you need to decide what weight ranges you want to set and how much to charge for each of them. In this recipe we will configure three weight ranges as shown in the following table:

Weight range	Cost
Up to 0.99kg	£3.00
1kg - 1.99kg	£5.00
2kg and heavier	£7.50

So, our 0.25kg DVDs would cost a minimum of £3.00 to deliver. And we could get up to three delivered together for that same price (3 * 0.25 = 0.75 < 0.99). But as soon as we add a fourth DVD, the weight is 1kg and that would slip into the second category and be charged at £5.00 And as soon as we add the eighth DVD and the weight will be 2kg, the cost will become £7.50 and any extra DVDs added after that will remain at the same shipping cost.

How to do it...

We will do this in two main phases because there are two tabs to configure. Then repeat and rinse as required. That is, for each weight range we will configure a shipment method that describes it clearly to the customer and defines the weight range to VirtueMart. Then, when the customers clicks on their cart, they will see an explanation of the shipment method they qualify for and of course, how much it will cost.

Use the Shipment Method Information tab and perform the following steps:

1. From the VirtueMart control panel click on the **Shop** menu and then **Shipment Methods**. You will be presented with a blank page if you haven't configured any shipment methods yet. So let's configure one.

2. Click on **New** from the row of buttons on the screen.

3. First we will fill in the **Shipment Method Information** tab. The following screenshot is an example of the tab:

4. **Shipment Name** is the title of the shipment method as it will appear to your customers and in your control panel to you. Hence, enter something simple and as concise as possible in the **Shipment Name** field.

5. **Published** means do you want this shipment method to be used? Select **Yes**.

6. **Shipment Description** is an actual explanation that will appear in the shopping cart to the customer when their basket matches the criteria in the shipment option we will configure.

7. The **Shipment Method** dropdown will allow you to select other shipment modules that can be purchased and installed. Before you buy anything be sure to see just how much you can do with what is already installed as standard.

8. Leave the **Shipment Method** dropdown on **By Weight, Zip and Countries**.

9. For **Shopper Group** choose **Select all options**. The **List Order** field allows you to decide in which order the shipping options are presented to your customers.

10. The previous step only really matters when more than one shipment option criteria is matched by the basket. That won't happen in this example so if 'by weight' is your first or only shipping choice, leave it at the default 0. If you have other options, choose where in the list you want this one to come. You will also have to select the position of the others as well from the specific shipment options **Shipment Methods Information** tab.

11. Click on **Save** and then move on to the **Configuration tab**.

12. The **Configuration** tab holds no nasty surprises either. Take a look at our configuration and then the explanation of what to do. The following screenshot describes the **Configuration** tab:

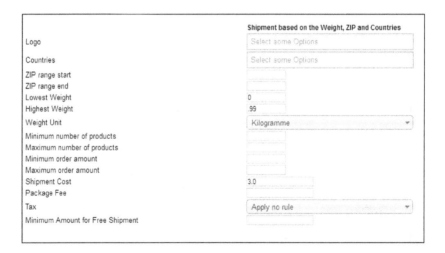

13. The only fields we need to worry about are **Lowest Weight** where we have entered 0 because that is the starting weight for our first weight range and in **Highest Weight** we entered 0.99, which is the heaviest basket that will qualify for this shipment option.

14. Then in **Shipment Cost** we have entered 3.0 because that is what the plan was to charge for this weight range.

15. Click on **Save and Close** and let's move on.

16. Now, in order to configure the second and third weight ranges, perform the exact same steps and only change the pertinent parts to match the next weight range in your plans.

17. So click on **New**. Here is our screen after configuring the **Shipment Method Information** tab for the second weight range. The following screenshot shows the parts that have changed:

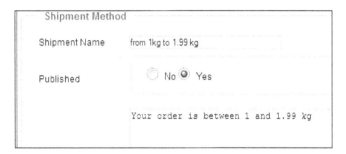

18. Quite simply we did exactly the same as before but entered the **Shipment Name** and **Shipment Description** to match the second weight range. Now for the **Configuration** tab refer the following screenshot:

19. So we entered the **Lowest Weight** as 1, the **Highest Weight** as 1.99 and the **Shipment Cost** as 5.0.

20. Click on **Save and Close**.

Do exactly the same with appropriate variations to create the last weight range. The only further difference could be that you should enter a very high weight that will probably never be achieved, like 50kg in the **Highest Weight** field. You could leave it empty and VirtueMart will use this option for anything over the starting weight. It is a good practice to enter a maximum weight however.

> If you have very finely grained weight variations in your products, then you will need more finely grained weight variations in your ranges as well. For example, if you also sell a DVD disc cleaning cloth that weighed 0.002 kg then it would be possible to have a basket that weighed 0.992 kg. This would not fall into any of the shipping ranges and the customer would end up with free delivery. This is not good.

How it works...

By telling VirtueMart what weight ranges and prices to charge along with simple meaningful descriptions and titles, we can inform our customers in a transparent and fair manner what it will cost them to have their order delivered.

Here is the basket in action after configuring the three weight ranges. See the difference between 1 DVD weighing in at 0.25kg, 4 totalling 1kg, and 20 totalling 5kg as shown in the following screenshot:

Configuring shipping by country, zone, or continent

In this recipe you will be able to assign a cost to a specific country. VirtueMart will automatically detect the country the customer wants the order delivered to and apply the appropriate charge.

Getting ready

Work out how much you want to charge for delivery and to which countries. The following table gives us the details as to what we will be configuring in the recipe but it would be trivial to change the countries and costs to suit us:

Country	Cost
United Kingdom	£2.00
EU members	£4.00
USA/Canada	£7.00
Outside US/Canada/Europe/EU	£10.00

How to do it...

The recipe works by defining costs either individually to a single country or to groups of countries. First up we will assign a single country and configure the cost.

In our example this is the UK, but it would work just as well for any country. It is quite a common configuration to have a low shipping cost for customers in the same country as the store:

1. Firstly, click on **Shipment Methods** in the **Shop** menu of VirtueMart.

2. Then click on **New** to add a shipping method. There are two tabs to configure, the first one is filled out and explained in the following screenshot:

3. Everything can be left on the default except the **Shipping Name** which we enter as UK and the **Shipping Description** where we enter To addresses in the UK.

4. You will shortly see that this name and description is used in the shopping cart to explain to customers what/why this shipping option has been selected for them.

5. Now, click on **Save** and then click on the **Configuration** tab.

6. As shown in the previous screenshot, we only need to configure two things. First click on the **Countries** field and search for and select **United Kingdom**.

7. Then in the **Package Fee** field enter 2.0 as per our plan for the shipping cost to this country. Click on **Save and Exit**.

8. Now click on the **New** button again and on the first tab we will enter the following **Shipment Name** and **Shipment Description**. Leave the **Published** radio button at the default **Yes**.

9. Click on **Save** to update the other tabs and then click on the **Configuration** tab.

10. Now this time we have a bit more work to do, but not too much. Enter the cost (4.0) in the **Shipping Cost** field.

11. This time we need to search for and select each of the individual EU member countries. This is tedious but it does give us a very fine control over who gets charged what.

 Make sure that in your plan, no countries are selected in more than one configuration as this will present the customer with an unnecessary option that could cause confusion and an abandoned cart.

Based on the previous tip we will not select the United Kingdom despite it being an EU member country (at time of writing at least) because the UK already has its own rate configured separately. After a bit of time on Wikipedia here is what I came up with.

12. Click on **Save and Exit**.

13. Now you just need to repeat the process for all the other zones/groups. Just change the description and the countries you select each time. And when it comes to the last group **Outside US/Canada/Europe/EU** simply select every country that you haven't already.

How it works...

By configuring multiple shipment options to cover all the scenarios required by your store VirtueMart will pick the right one based on the actual shipment address of the customers order.

Hopefully this recipe was as varied and deliberately convoluted enough to show you how to configure almost any combination of country, zone, or continent.

So add some products to your cart, click on the **View Cart** link, and then click on **Add/Edit Shipment Address**. Fill out an appropriate address to test the configuration. Then click on **Save**. You can test with a UK address as shown in the following screenshot:

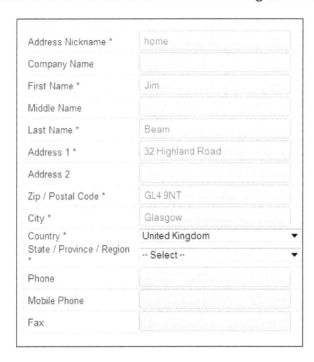

In the following screenshot you can see that VirtueMart is charging the correct amount for the correct reason:

	Product prices result	£40.00	£239.80
UK To addresses in the UK			£2.00

Try it out for any of the countries we configured. It just works. No complicated choices for the customer means more sales for you.

There's more...

Note that if you want your store to deliver to multiple countries and weight ranges, the configuration gets more complex. In addition you cannot define weight ranges without including countries and then simply configure countries and expect them to work independently. See the *Configuring shipping by a combination of criteria* recipe if you need to do this.

Configuring shipping by zip code

There are a lot of great VirtueMart shipping plug-ins. And if you want to do anything simple yet very specific like shipping by US state, Australian region, UK city, or similar, then the Joomla! extensions directory is the place to go. There is a solution to most common specific problems although most of the good ones are paid. However if you just want to configure by US zip code this recipe is for you..

 Not all the available shipping plugins are listed in the Joomla! extensions directory. They can also be found in the VirtueMart forum's third party extension section or at extensions.virtuemart.net.

Getting ready

Gather a list of zip code ranges to cover the states you are interested in. You will see the beginnings of a plan to cover the whole of the USA by proceeding alphabetically through the first three states. You can get approximate zip ranges by state from www.unitedstateszipcodes.org. The first three zip ranges are given in the following table:

State	Zip range	Cost
Alabama	35004 to 36925	$10.00
Alaska	99501 to 99950	$15.00
Arizona	85001 to 86556	$12.00

How to do it...

Let's start off by setting up **Alabama and other bordering states**.

1. Select the **Shop** menu and then click on **Shipment Method**.

2. Now, click on the **New** button. The following screenshot is the first tab configured for our "approximately Alabama" shipment method.

3. Not much to do here. Just a title for our method in the **Shipment Name** field, **Alabama**, and a description in the **Shipment Description** field, as we discussed earlier.

4. Click on **Save** and then select the **Configuration** tab. The tab can be seen in the following screenshot:

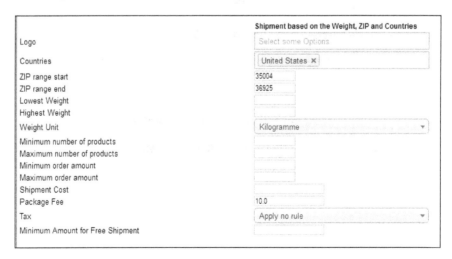

5. Just four fields we need to fill out. Click on **Countries** and search for **United States** and then select it.

6. Enter the start and end of the zip range in **Zip Range Start** and **Zip Range End**. Then lastly, enter the price **10.0** in the **Package Fee** field.

7. Click on **Save and Exit**.

8. Click **New** again and do the same as before but just vary the **Shipment Name**, **Shipment Description**, **Zip Range Start**, **Zip Range End**, and **Package Fee** to suit the details in the table in the _Getting ready_ section of this recipe.

How it works...

The customer's zip from their delivery address is matched to one of the shipping option rules and the appropriate price for shipping is charged.

Here a customer enters an Arizona zip code in their delivery details.

In the following screenshot, you see the appropriate charge being applied on the cart page:

There's more...

How VirtueMart zip codes work?

The way you implement a zip code strategy is by configuring a price for a range of codes. For example, starting with "A", the zip codes in Alabama run from 35004 to 36925. It is important to mention although it is nothing to be concerned about really, that zip codes often cross state borders. So if we define Alabama with the code range mentioned then it is almost inevitable that someone from a surrounding state will have what our system considers an Alabama zip code.

This is not a problem as long as we don't cause confusion. If you think about the purpose for this process, simply to set a shipping price then this method is good enough. The chances of the actual cost to us varying just because a property is fairly nearby over the state line is not realistic. So we can merrily configure our states but make sure we present them in a way that doesn't confuse. If you need more precision you can go through the zip code lists and define multiple ranges for each state but if you are going to be so precise then you are better off going for a shipping by state plug-in or a plug-in that handles your preferred carrier and let them worry about the details.

So assuming this method is "good enough" for you, we could for example describe all our VirtueMart shipment method descriptions that our customers see as "State Name and other bordering states". So a shopper in Mississippi seeing **Alabama and other bordering states** will probably accept that our system has got it right and proceed to part with their money.

It should all become clear as we proceed and test.

Configuring shipping by a combination of criteria

The most important thing to get right when setting up shipping for any e-commerce store is planning. The main considerations should be what makes sense to your customers, accuracy of the charge, and simplicity. That is, the best configuration for an e-commerce shipping setup is the simplest one that charges the right amount in a way your customers understand.

Having said that, some setups will be necessarily complex. What about the zip code scenario in the previous recipe? Now consider if the charge should change by weight as well? We can quite simply configure multiple shipping options per zip range that take into account a different weight range each. There comes a point, as mentioned twice already, where a custom shipping plug-in will be the best solution. But buying a plugin is not always the best solution and this recipe will configure a somewhat complex setup with the standard VirtueMart shipping options.

The aim of the recipe is to configure shipping by multiple countries and weight ranges. For brevity we will look at a setup that serves the USA and Canada with two weight ranges but this could easily be expanded to include as many countries and weight ranges as you like.

If you want help to configure more complex country scenarios such as economic zones or continents at the same time then the *Configuring shipping by country, zone or continent* recipe would be a good introduction to this recipe.

Here we will stick to the following plan.

Getting ready

Let's define what we will set out to achieve lest we become mesmerized by a sea of weights, countries, and shipping methods.

We will set up shipping to the USA and Canada and to each a different price for orders weighing up to and over 10kg.

Country	Weight range	Cost
USA	Up to 10kg	$10.00
Canada	Up to 10kg	$15.00
USA	>10kg	$12.00
Canada	>10kg	$17.00

How to do it...

When we present things nice and clearly the complexity starts to disappear. We can clearly see that all we need is four shipping options as defined previously. So let's get configuring.

1. From the **Shop** menu, select **Shipment Methods** and then click on **New**. Here we will configure the first option from the previous for USA up to 10kg at $10. The following screenshot shows us how to configure the first tab of this first shipment option:

2. In the next screen, we enter the information including the **Shipment Name** as **USA** and the **Shipment Description**, which further defines the option for our customers. Set this as **up to 10kg**.

3. Click on the **Configuration** tab and we will quickly configure it.

	Shipment based on the Weight, ZIP and Countries
Logo	Select some Options
Countries	United States ×
ZIP range start	
ZIP range end	
Lowest Weight	
Highest Weight	10.0
Weight Unit	Kilogramme
Minimum number of products	
Maximum number of products	
Minimum order amount	
Maximum order amount	
Shipment Cost	10
Package Fee	
Tax	Apply no rule
Minimum Amount for Free Shipment	

4. As you can see we need to select **United States** in the **Countries** field, **10.0** in the **Highest Weight** field and **10** in the **Shipment Cost** field.

5. If you are wondering why we didn't enter anything in the **Lowest Weight** field it is because leaving it blank is the same as zero. Click on **Save and Exit**.

6. Now select the newly created shipment option in the main Shipment Method page by checking its selection box as shown in the following screenshot:

7. Click on the **Clone Shipment** button and then click on the newly cloned (copied) shipment option. Now simply amend the details as follows.

    1. On the first tab change **USA copy** to **USA**. Change the **Shipment Description** to **over 10kg**.

    2. On the **Configuration** tab enter 10.001 in the **Lowest Weight** field and change the **Highest Weight** to 999 or some weight that will never be exceeded in your store.

    3. Click on **Save and Exit**.

We now have two shipment options both for the USA, one for orders up to 10kg and one for orders over. Let's do some more cloning.

8. Select the check boxes of both the USA shipment options and click **Clone Shipment**. Now click into each in turn and set both **Shipment Title** fields to **Canada** and on each of the **Configuration** tabs **Country** field, delete **United States** and select **Canada**. Remember to click on **Save and Exit** each when done.

We are done now. The following screenshot shows how the Shipment Method page will look now:

How it works...

By combining countries and weights in shipping options, VirtueMart will now offer a more granular shipping cost escalation to multiple countries and by multiple weights of order. The following screenshot is an order to the USA under 10kg (left) and an order to Canada over 10kg (right):

Configuring VAT on the entire purchase (including or excluding VAT on delivery costs)

This recipe shows you how to configure a basic Value Added Tax. After careful consultation with your tax lawyer/accountant here is how you implement a rate of 20 percent VAT on the entire customer purchase including delivery.

Getting ready

Consult with a tax lawyer/accountant if your VAT rate should be added onto delivery or not.

How to do it...

As usual we will see that taken a step at a time there is nothing complex about this type of shipping configuration:

1. From the **Products** menu select **Taxes and Calculation Rules**. Now click on **New**. Configure the Tax and Calculation Rule page like the following:

Enter or select the following values for the corresponding fields.

Field	Value to enter/select
Calculation Rule name	20% VAT
Published	check
Type of Arithmetic Operation	**VAT tax per product**
Math Operation	+%
Value	20.0
Currency	**British pound** (Or your main store currency)
Visible for Shopper	**Yes**
Start Date	Leave blank to auto select today.
End Date	Leave blank to auto select never end.

2. Click on **Save** then go and check out the 20% being added to your customers carts.

    In many situations, like in the UK when you are liable for VAT, you will need to charge VAT on delivery also. This is straightforward. If your tax professional says you do not need to charge VAT on delivery you can skip this section.

3. Click on **Shipment Methods** from the **Shop** menu. Click on the first shipment method that you need to charge VAT on.

4. Click on the **Configuration** tab. Then, scroll down until you see the following screenshot:

5. Click on the **Tax** drop-down selector and choose the tax rule we just created **20% VAT**.

6. Click on **Save and Exit** and repeat for each shipment option that you need to charge VAT on.

How it works...

By creating a rule in the VirtueMart database VAT at 20 percent will now be added and displayed on each cart and invoice created by VirtueMart.

Configuring a tax to start or finish on a set date

In most countries tax rates vary. For example in the UK there is a "special" 20 percent VAT rate which is set to expire on December 31, 2013 when the old VAT rate of 17 percent will hopefully rematerialize. We can plan forward for this.

Getting ready

Consult with a tax lawyer/accountant.

Get the dates and rates of tax. Then we will implement them using the examples mentioned in the book.

How to do it...

Create two tax rules using the *Configuring VAT on the entire purchase (including or excluding VAT on delivery costs)* recipe if necessary. One at the current rate and the other at the new future rate. You may have already implemented one of them previously.

> You can use this recipe to modify the start and end dates for any of the tax rules implemented in this book. We use the *Configuring VAT on the entire purchase (including or excluding VAT on delivery costs)* recipe as an example only because it fits the scenario described. When you implement the second tax note, by default it is live immediately. If your store is actually trading, then implement the next steps immediately or uncheck the **Published** checkbox (does not have a tick in it) and remember to check it (does have a tick in it) when you implement the date or it will not start.

Perform the following steps to configure the end date to the current tax:

1. On the Taxes and Calculation rules page (list), click on **current tax** and scroll down to the following:

2. Select the date the day before the new tax begins. In this case, it is December 31, 2013. The dates are inclusive so this will run until the midnight of December 31, 2013 as shown in the following screenshot:

3. Click on **Save and Exit**.

4. On the Taxes and Calculation rules page (list), click on the future tax option that we configured and make sure that the **Published** check box is checked (has a tick in it). Scroll down to the **Start Date** widget then click on it.

5. Select the actual date on which the new tax begins. In this case, January 1, 2014. The dates are inclusive so this will start at the very first minute of 2014 immediately after the old one expires, as shown in the following screenshot:

6. Click on **Save and Exit**.

How it works...

By setting up two taxes, one active with the current tax rate but with an end date (the day before the new one starts), and then the other one with a start date (the day it is due to start with the new rate) and no end date, Now your store will seamlessly implement the correct tax rate changing all the cart references to it as well as customer invoices.

Configuring a tax on a per-category basis

Configuring a tax on a per category basis works when you have a category or sub category of products that attracts a different VAT rate from your regular store rate, and we want this tax to only affect the specific category it is applied to.

Getting ready

Consult a tax lawyer/accountant.

How to do it...

For the purposes of demonstration we will implement a 40 percent tax on CMS movies. E-commerce and other DVDs, however, are still charged at the regular tax rate by this new tax introduced by the government of the day:

1. On the Taxes and Calculation rules page (list), click on the **New** button. The following table gives details of the values to configure. All the unmentioned fields can be left as their default:

Field	Value to enter/select
Calculation Rule name	`40 percent VAT`
Published	check
Description	Write something to remind you of the reason for this rule (for example, "Unfair tax on innocent CMS DVD purchasers.")
Type of Arithmetic Operation	**VAT tax per product**
Math Operation	+%
Value	`40.0`
Currency	**British pound** (or your main store currency)
Product Category	Select the category this rate applies to (in this case the CMS Movies category).

Field	Value to enter/select
Visible for Shopper	Yes
Start Date	Leave blank to auto select today
End Date	Leave blank to auto select never end

2. Click on **Save and Exit**. Now if you have a default "catch all" tax rule as mentioned in the *Configuring VAT on the entire purchase (including or excluding VAT on delivery costs)* recipe, then you need to set that rule to include all categories except the one the new rate applies to. In this example that means just the E-commerce DVDs category. Otherwise CMS DVD customers will have a whopping two taxes applied.

3. On the **Taxes and Calculation rules page** (list), click on the default overall tax rule and scroll down to the **Product Category** field as shown in the following screenshot:

Product Category	E-Commerce Movies ✕

4. Choose all the categories not included in the new rule. In this example that's the **E-Commerce Movies** category.

5. Click on **Save and Close**.

How it works...

Here you can see in your store that the appropriate tax rate is being applied to the appropriate categories.

4
Making Your Store Look Amazing

In this chapter we will cover:

- ▸ Removing the Joomla! branding at the footer
- ▸ Installing a VirtueMart template
- ▸ Installing a Joomla! template
- ▸ Creating and installing a template with Artisteer design software
- ▸ Installing the Warp framework/template
- ▸ Installing the Gantry framework/template
- ▸ Customizing the Gantry framework/template
- ▸ Uninstalling a template
- ▸ Cool header banners with jQuery and Sourcerer

Introduction

Looks are everything on the web. If your store doesn't look enticing and professional to your customers then everything else is a waste. This chapter looks at how to make your VirtueMart look stunning.

There are many different approaches to creating a hot-looking store. The one that is best for you or your client will depend upon your budget and your skill set.

The recipes in this chapter will cater to all budgets and skill sets. For example, we will cover the very simple task of finding and installing a free Joomla! template or installing a VirtueMart theme.

Then we will look at the pros and cons of using two different professional frameworks namely Warp and Gantry.

In the middle of all this, we will also look at the stunningly versatile Artisteer design software that won't quite give you the perfect professional job but does a very fine job of letting you choose just about every aspect of your design without any CSS/coding skills.

Removing the Joomla! branding at the footer

With each version of Joomla! and VirtueMart being better than the last one in terms of looks and performance, it is not unheard of to launch your store with the default looks of Joomla! and VirtueMart.

The least you will probably want to do is remove the **Powered by Joomla!®** link at the footer of your store. This will make your store appear entirely your own and perhaps have a minor benefit to SEO as well by removing the outbound link.

Getting ready

Log in to your Joomla! control panel. This recipe was tested using the **Beez_20** template but should work on any template where the same message appears. We will also be using the Firefox web browser search function but again, this is almost identical in other browsers.

Identify the message to be removed on the frontend of your site as shown in the following screenshot:

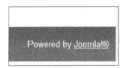

How to do it...

This is going to be nice and easy so let's get started and perform the following steps:

1. Navigate to **Extensions | Template Manager** from the main Joomla! drop-down menu as shown in the following screenshot:

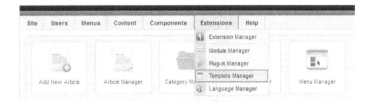

2. Now click on the **Templates** link (it is the one next door to the **Styles** link) as shown in the following screenshot:

3. Scroll down until you see **Beez_20 details and Files** click on it as shown in the following screenshot:

4. Now scroll down and click on **Edit main page template**.

5. Next press *Ctrl +F* on your keyboard to bring up the Firefox search bar and enter `<div id="footer">` as your search term. Firefox will present you with the following code:

```
<div id="footer">

        <jdoc:include type="modules" name="position-14" />

        <p>
                <?php echo JText::_('TPL_BEEZ2_POWERED_BY'); ?> <a href="http://www.joomla.org/">Joomla!&#174;</a>
        </p>
</div><!-- end footer -->
```

6. Delete everything between `<p>` and `</p>` both inclusive.

7. Click on **Save & Close**.

How it works...

Check your Joomla! home page. We now have a nice clean and empty footer. We can add Joomla! and VirtueMart modules or just leave it empty.

Installing a VirtueMart template

In this recipe we will look at how to install a theme to make your store look great with a couple of clicks. There are a few things to consider first. Is your website just a store? That is, are all your pages going to be VirtueMart pages?

If the answer is yes then this is definitely the recipe for you. Alternatively you might just have a few shop pages in amongst an extensive Joomla! based content site. If this is the case then you might be better off installing a Joomla! template and then setting VirtueMart to use that. If this describes your situation then the next recipe, *Installing a Joomla! template* is more appropriate for you.

And there is a third option as well. You have content pages and a large number of VirtueMart pages. In this situation some experimentation and planning is required. You will either need to choose a Joomla! template that you are happy with for everything or a Joomla! template and a VirtueMart theme which look good together. Or you could use two templates. This last scenario is covered in the *Creating and installing a template with Artisteer design software* recipe.

Getting ready

Find a template which is either free or paid and download the files from the template provider's site (they will be in the form of a single compressed archive) on your computer. The *Appendix. Apps, VirtueMart, and Joomla! Resources* might be of some help here.

How to do it...

Installing a VirtueMart template has never been as easy as it is in VirtueMart 2. Perform the following steps for the same:

1. Navigate to **Extensions | Extension Manager** from the top Joomla! menu.

2. Click on the **Browse...** button in the **Upload Package File** area, find and select your template file as shown in the following screenshot:

3. Click on the **Upload & Install** button and you are done!

How it works...

The VirtueMart template is now installed. Take a look at your shiny new store.

Installing a Joomla! Template

As there is clearly something of a supply problem when it comes to VirtueMart-specific free templates, this recipe will look at installing a regular Joomla! template and using it in your VirtueMart store.

Installing a Joomla! template is a very easy thing to do. But if you have never done it before read on.

Getting ready

Check the resources appendix for a choice of places to get free and paid templates. Download your chosen template on your desktop. It should be in the form of a ZIP file. Log in to your Joomla! admin area and read on.

How to do it...

This simple recipe is in two steps. First we upload the template then we set it as the active template.

1. Select **Extensions | Extension Manager** from the top Joomla! menu.

2. Click on the **Browse...** button in the **Upload Package File** area, find and select your template file as shown in the following screenshot:

3. Click on the **Upload & Install** button.

4. Now select **Extensions | Template Manager**.

5. Click on the checkbox of the template you just installed and then click on **Make Default**.

How it works...

So what we did was to install the template through the usual Joomla! installation mechanism and once the template was installed we simply told Joomla! to use it. That's it. You can now go and assign all your modules to your new template.

Creating and installing a template with an Artisteer design software

I don't normally like to recommend one commercial solution over another. Mainly because I don't want to be held responsible for the vagaries and consistencies of a product or service and also because there are almost always pros and cons between the different product and service providers.

However Artisteer is a bit different. They have been around for years, the product does exactly what it says it does and there isn't really any alternative - the product is unique.

Artisteer is like having a CSS guru inside your PC. You can click on and choose from the whole site layout options to tiny button and tab configurations. You can even add Flash and pretty nifty scrolling banners and so on. We will do the latter in a minute.

 Excessive use of these features raises the possibility of JavaScript conflicts with VirtueMart. Add a feature at a time and test regularly.

It is certainly true that you probably won't end up with a design as good as something bespoke that you pay a professional design studio for, but this recipe is for those of you who need a totally unique bespoke design for a bit over $100. The benefit over a bespoke design service is that you can use it for as many designs as you like and that Artisteer won't complain if you ask for extra design revisions over the agreed amount.

Getting ready

It always helps to have ideas in your mind. Look at competitor sites and other Joomla!/ VirtueMart sites to have an idea of the colors and styles that you like. Artisteer is sure to have something similar.

Also, try and consider the best general layout for your site such as single or multiple columns. This will prevent you from going round in circles with the vast array of options that Artisteer is about to throw at us. Perhaps do a sketch on a paper.

You need have all the images that you want to use in the design on your desktop.

If you will have several different layouts, perhaps one for the home page and a different one for subpages/shop then that's fine. We will look at how to do this in Artisteer. Download and install the standard edition trial from `http://www.artisteer.com/?p=downloads`.

Obviously your design ideas will be quite different from the ones demonstrated in the book. But it should be trivial to adapt my specific instructions to suit your design.

Most likely you will want to spend a good amount of time wading through and sampling the different options that Artisteer offers. That's fine, I will just whiz through for now and we should have an acceptable design in minutes.

How to do it...

This recipe is quite a long one, but step-by-step there is nothing overly complicated in this at all. If you find yourself itching to customize a bit further in any of the upcoming steps that is absolutely fine and is encouraged. Fire up Artisteer and let's start making our site.

1. Your first choice on starting Artisteer is to choose your starting point. You can either select from a preconfigured template or a blank one as shown in the following screenshot:

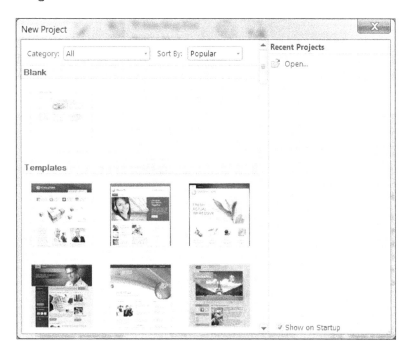

2. For the purposes of following this recipe precisely, choose the **Blank** template.

3. From the top Artisteer menu select the **Colors & Fonts** tab as shown in the following screenshot:

4. Select the **Colors and Themes** drop down and select the theme you like. We have chosen **Ice Water** under the **Sky Blue** menu in the example.

5. Now that we have decided on a color theme, let's choose the font set. Click on the **Font Set** dropdown and choose a set of fonts to compliment the colors and your products. We chose the **Salient** font set because, it gives a clean modern-ish sans serif look.

6. Finally click on **Font Scale** and choose **120** percentage because the default salient size is a little small.

7. Now select the **Menu** tab and click on the **Menu Area** dropdown, and then click on **Fill**. Choose a smart menu fill color as shown in the following screenshot:

8. Click on the text **Enter Site Title** and enter the name of your store. In the example, we put the store name as The Joomla DVD Store.

9. You are probably beginning to notice that just about every aspect of every element can be changed in a vast number of ways. Just one more change and then we can wrap up the main page. Click on the **Header** tab. We will make a smart rotating banner in just a few clicks.

10. In order to make a banner, find and click on the **New Slide** button as shown in the following screenshot:

11. Here, as you can see the slides of your rotating banners can be an image you already own or custom designed in Artisteer from a blank page. Click on **Blank**. Do this for as many number of slides and whatever types you want.

12. Now you can see that you can select from slides one through three by clicking on the navigation circles. Click on them in turn to see it flip between slides as shown in the following screenshot:

13. Click on the first navigation circle. Let's define a background. If you chose a picture for your slide then you don't need to do this bit. Now click on the **Background Image** dropdown and choose something cool for the first slide.

14. Select the second navigation circle, choose a background and repeat the same procedure for all your slides. Let's choose images from the **Wind Glass** section in the **Background Image** dropdown.

15. Watch a preview of your slide show by clicking on the **Play** button in the **Slide Show** section of the main Artisteer tool bar.

16. Now let's make the remaining content our own. Right-click on any images you want to change and select **Change Image** from the list of options. Browse to and choose the image to be replaced.

17. Right-click on all links and select either **Remove Hyperlink** (if you do not need it) or **Edit Hyperlink** (to change the text and the target).

18. Click on any text you want to edit and type your descriptions.

Designing your store pages

Since this is for an e-commerce focused VirtueMart site we will do things a little differently than usual in order to design your own pages using the Artisteer method.

We are going to further adapt this template and make it an entirely new and then when we upload, it we will assign it to just the VirtueMart menus. This way we have a perfectly matching design but with different features in the store. Perform the following steps:

1. Export the template as it is. It will serve as the default Joomla! template. Navigate to **File | Export | Joomla! Template**. Select the correct version of Joomla! and set the **Positions** dropdown to **position-1, position-2...** .Make sure to check the boxes **Zip Archive** and **Include content**. Set the **File Name:** to ArtisteerDefault as shown in the following screenshot:

 If you have purchased Artisteer, then you can select **File | Save as** and name the file ArtisteerDefault. Now save the project again as ArtisteerVM. You can now make the changes you want on just store pages from here. You will then be able to revisit any aspect of either template and re-export it at your leisure.

2. Now we will make some quick adaptations for the VM version of the template. Let's get rid of the extraneous menus. Hover over the block titled **VMenu** on the left-hand side. Find the tiny delete icon as shown in the following screenshot, second from the left after the light bulb icon:

3. Click on it, the block is gone. In the block titled **Block** edit the title and text to be a welcome message to your store. Something like the following screenshot:

4. Make any other changes you want on the store but not the main Joomla! template.

5. We now have two templates, `ArtisteerDefault` and `ArtisteerVM`. Here is what you need to do. Log in to your Joomla! admin panel and from the main Joomla! menu select **Extensions | Extension Manager**.

6. In the **Upload Package File** area, browse to the first template file and select it. Now click on **Upload & Install**. Wait for the install to complete. Do the same for the other template files. Wait for the install to complete. It doesn't matter which order you do it in.

7. Now select **Extensions | Template Manager**. You should see the two templates you just installed as shown in the following screenshot:

☐	🖼	ArtisteerDefault - Default
☐	🖼	ArtisteerVM - Default

8. Check the box for **ArtisteerDefault** and click on the **Make Default** button. Now click on the **ArtisteerDefault** link to go to its **Template Manager: Edit Style** page. Press the button on the right-labeled **Import Content from Template**, then click on **Import** and finally **Continue**.

9. Now click on the **ArtisteerVM** template to go to its **Template Manager: Edit Style** page.

10. Click on the right-labeled **Import Content from Template**, then click on **Import** and then **Continue**. Scroll down to the **Menus Assignment** area and check the checkbox for **Shop**. Click on **Save and Close**.

11. We are really close now. We just need to add in some of our VirtueMart modules to these templates and we are done here. Select **Extensions | Module Manager** from the main Joomla! menu.

12. We want to add the VM Category module to **position-7** and the shopping cart module to **position-7**.

13. Find and click on the **VM - Category** module.

14. Click on the **Select Position** button and select **position-7**.

15. Scroll down to the **Menu Assignment** area and click on the **Module Assignment** dropdown and choose **On All Pages**.

16. Click on **Save and Close**.

17. Do exactly the same as discussed from step 13 to 15 for the **VM - Shopping Cart** module and any others you want to show.

How it works...

Our finished site product page is as shown in the following screenshot:

The home page is as shown in the following screenshot:

Artisteer might make all but the best web designers around the world lose a little sleep and it will definitely please many with its flexibility, features, and cost as demonstrated.

There's more...

It is true that the simple difference between the two templates could have been implemented by not deploying the Artisteer generated modules in the VirtueMart area and a more realistic example might have been to have a product focused header instead of the generic one on the VM template. But the example works for demonstration purposes.

Installing the Warp framework/template

The Warp framework is created by YOOtheme. If you like working with this template, check out their fancier offerings on www.yootheme.com.

Advantages and disadvantages of using Warp

Warp extensions just work and are in my opinion unrivalled. If you are happy with the default theme used in this recipe or you like one of their themes from the YOOtheme website, then you are most likely to be satisfied.

You can also modify the Warp framework templates but only with a good knowledge of CSS/ HTML and a bit of inside information about the framework as well.

If on the other hand you feel the need to make adjustments to columns, colors, fonts, and much more without any CSS/HTML knowledge, then check the next two recipes that cover a competitor framework called Gantry.

Getting ready

Head over to `http://www.yootheme.com/demo/joomla` and click on the **Master Theme** download icon as shown in the following screenshot:

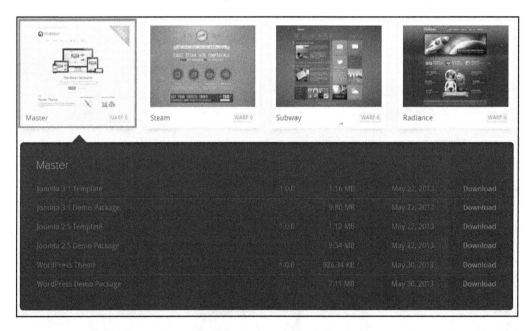

Click on the **download** button for your version of Joomla! and save it on your desktop.

How to do it...

The Warp theme takes just a few clicks to install and as we will see, it is well worth it. So let's do it.

1. In the Joomla! control panel choose **Extensions | Extension Manager** from the top drop-down menu.

2. Now click on **Browse...** in the **Upload Package File** area, select the file `yoo_master_jxx.zip` that you just downloaded on your desktop and click on **Upload & Install** as shown in the following screenshot:

3. We can now see the following screenshot:

4. Now we will switch to the framework/master theme. Navigate to **Extensions | Template Manager**. Select the check-box next to **yoo_master - Default** as shown in the following screenshot:

5. Click on **Make Default** in the top row of buttons.

How it works...

The Warp framework and all its advantages are now installed. If you view your site/store, you will see that all the modules have disappeared. In the next recipe *Customizing the Warp framework*, we will get them back again as well as make some customizations.

Before you start to wonder what all this was for, resize your browser on the screen to about the size of a mobile phone or small tablet. You can see a significant advantage to the Warp framework compared to Joomla! 2.5 default themes.

The product page before the Wrap framework is not so good. We can see that the entire contents of the screen are just a squashed up mess as shown in the following screenshot:

With the Wrap framework, we have a responsive UI as shown in the following screenshot:

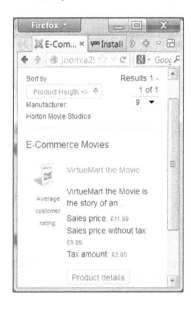

As we can see, the responsive (to screen size) framework of Warp has formatted our content really well, even on a mobile phone sized screen!

Installing the Gantry framework/template

Gantry is extraordinarily configurable without coding, unlike the Warp framework and like the Warp framework, as we will see it is highly responsive to different screen sizes. So Gantry is ideally suited for the non-technical person, who wants a responsive website as well as making some simple customizations that make our site unique.

Getting ready

Download the framework for free from `http://www.gantry-framework.org/download`. Be sure to get the right one for your version of Joomla!.

When you have chosen your version of Joomla! you are faced with a few choices as shown in the following screenshot:

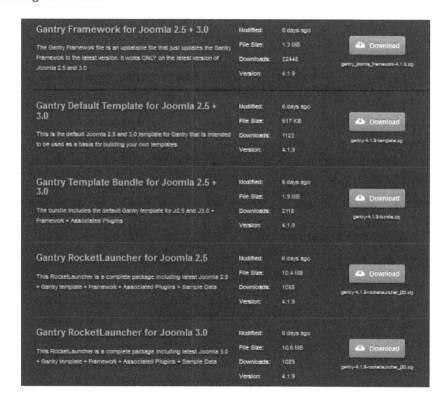

We need the Gantry template bundle for Joomla! x.x where x.x matches our version of Joomla!. Click on the **Download** button.

After getting it on your desktop, read on.

How to do it...

The Gantry framework like the Warp framework is well worth the few minutes it will take to install. Also, when we are done, be sure to take a look at how to configure it easily in the next recipe.

1. From your Joomla! control panel select **Extensions | Extension Manager**.

2. Click on the **Browse...** button and select your recent Gantry download, `gantry-4.x.x-bundle.zip` or similar.

3. Now click on **Upload & install**.

4. Almost done. Navigate to **Extensions | Template Manager** from the top Joomla! menu.

5. Put a tick in the box to the left of **Gantry - Default** as shown in the following screenshot:

6. Click on **Make Default** in the top row of buttons.

How it works...

The theme is now fully installed with the sample content for us to experiment with in the next recipe. The process apart from finding and choosing the files was nearly identical to a regular Joomla! template but how your site now performs is a little different.

Try resizing your browser or visiting your site from a mobile phone as shown in the following screenshot:

See how the menu implementation changes to mobile-friendly and the module arrangement just pops up to a neat column instead of being spread across the page and causing us to scroll down just to see the right-hand side. Joomla! 3.x does this almost as well using the Bootstrap framework. But alas, at the time of writing, VirtueMart is not compatible with Joomla! 3.

However the real advantage of Gantry over other modern Joomla! compatible frameworks such as Warp is how easily we can customize it to make it our own. That's covered in the *Customizing the Gantry framework/template* recipe.

See also

▸ The *Installing the Warp framework/template* recipe

Customizing the Gantry framework/template

We will go through configuring all the main Gantry options. Follow along exactly or vary what you do at various stages to end up with a different result.

Getting ready

See the previous *Installing the Gantry framework/template* recipe.

How to do it...

As mentioned at the start of this recipe, what makes Gantry different from other frameworks is the extent to which we can customize the look of our template without a single line of code. Let's make some customizations now as shown in the following steps:

1. Navigate to **Extensions | Template Manager** and click on the **Gantry - Default** link. Select the **Overview** tab.

2. First we are going to choose a preset. That is one of the preconfigured starting points from which we will begin customization. Click on the **Presets** button in the row of buttons near the top of the page. You will see a cool drop-down of preset configurations to choose from as shown in the following screenshot:

3. Let's choose **Preset 4** because it is light with blue elements. Nice. Now we can do some tweaking. Click on **Save** and check out your site so that you know where you are starting your customizations from.

4. Now select the **Style** tab.

5. Let's put our own logo in place of the Gantry one. In the row of controls labeled **Logo**, select the **Type** drop-down and select **Custom**. We now have these options in the **Custom Logo** row as shown in the following screenshot:

6. Click on the **Select** button and then the **Browse...** button and choose your logo from your PC hard drive. Now click on **Start Upload**. Note that you might need to scroll down a bit to reveal the **Start Upload** button. Select the thumbnail image of the logo you just uploaded and click on **Insert**. Check your new logo on your store.

7. Now we can configure the color of all our links. Click on the colored square (Next to the label **Link Color**) which shows the current color and up pops this color chooser as shown in the following screenshot:

8. Choose the new color for your links by choosing the color range from the vertical color bar and the precise color from the resulting color square.

9. Finally on this tab we can choose a range of fonts from the **Font Family** dropdown. Try different fonts to find the one that looks good. Click on **Save** each time before you check the shop front. Try choosing the **Coda Caption** font family.

10. Now, click on the **Features** tab.

11. The top-five features on this tab are brilliant if you are setting up shop for a client. Every client will want a different combination of these features. It can be time consuming finding the code/module to add or switch these features off. Gantry lays it all out bare on a single page. We will try for as many features as possible, hence we will switch all the first five features to **ON** as shown in the following screenshot:

12. Click on **Save** and have a look at the effect on your store front as shown in the following screenshot:

13. After performing the previous steps, the following effects can be seen:

- **1**—a dynamic date that changes each day making your content appear fresh
- **2**—visitor changeable text size buttons so that people with different screen sizes and eyesight can set the text to suit them
- **3**—it provides credits to the theme designer
- **5**—it provides the copyright information
- **4**—it gives a cool button to jump to the top of the site and save our scrolling fingers from having to do it with the mouse scroll wheel.

14. Now lick the Menu tab.

15. Here you can determine the type of experience your visitors will have from the mobile devices. Click on the dropdown in the **Responsive Menu** field. Choose **Select Box** for the style of menu shown in the following screenshot when browsing on small screen devices:

The Layouts tab

The layouts tab only makes sense to configure once you have a plan for your module positions and you have some content, articles, and so on. So we will look at it generically.

This tab allows you to select the number of module places and/or the shape of the module layouts in a specific section of the template. Play with the settings and if you have the Joomla! sample content installed, you will see how the click of a box can give you a whole new layout.

The Advanced tab

1. Click the **Advanced** tab.

2. The best option on this tab is the **Load Transition** option as shown in the following screenshot:

3. Click on **ON**, and select **Save**, go and refresh a page in your store (*F5* on your keyboard). Watch the sweet fade-in effect which smoothens the loading of page elements. The effect is the same in most browsers.

4. Now, click on the **Assignments** tab and you will see the following screenshot:

Content / Horizontal Menu	Content / Special Menu
☑ Home	☑ Special Blog Page
☑ Contact Us	☑ Special Single Page
Content / Vertical Menu	**Main Menu**
☑ Home	☑ Home
☑ Contact Us	☑ Shop
Our Shop	
☑ About Us	

5. We want this template in use for every area of our Joomla! site and VirtueMart store. Hence, we have checked every box as you can see in the previous screenshot. Click on **Save** and we are done.

How it works...

The Gantry framework is highly customizable without touching the CSS, JavaScript, or the PHP code. It is possible to create a fairly unique layout and a reasonably personalized color scheme without even buying a Gantry template. It must be said however that the RocketTheme templates which are all Gantry templates are some of the hottest non-bespoke templates around.

Uninstalling a Joomla! template

You might have tried out a few of the template recipes. What will start to happen is that the content you installed from one will carry over and spoil the content from another.

Not to mention that you might have assigned certain links to another template altogether and the whole situation becomes a muddle.

The clean thing to do is only have templates you are actually using installed at any given time. This recipe will show you how to uninstall a template.

Getting ready

Log in to your Joomla! control panel.

How to do it...

We will now, very quickly remove an unwanted template. Repeat this recipe for each of the templates you will not be using as shown in the following steps:

1. Select **Extensions | Extension Manager**.

2. Click on the **Manage** tab as shown in the following screenshot:

3. Now you are on the **Extension Manager: Manage** page. From the row of dropdowns. We will click on the **Select Type** dropdown and choose **Templates** as shown in the following screenshot:

4. Now we can see a list of all your installed templates. Put a tick in the checkbox to the left of any templates you need to uninstall and click on the **Uninstall** button with the bin icon. You can see we just have the **Bluestork** admin template and the one other on your left as shown in the following screenshot:

How it works...

Using the friendly Joomla! template manager we have quickly and painlessly uninstalled all our unwanted templates.

Now you should be able to install any template from any recipe without annoying effects from the previously installed templates. You can also practice good template housekeeping by only having the templates that you need installed.

Cool header banners with jQuery and Sourcerer

Sourcerer is one of the most versatile add-ons for Joomla!. It allows us to add code (JavaScript, CSS, HTML, and PHP) just about anywhere in our website without editing a single file. This is useful in many ways and they are explored in detail in *Chapter 7, Extending Joomla! and VirtueMart*. But this recipe fits here nicely because we can significantly enhance the appearance of our store by using Sourcerer to add some JQuery magic and implement some cool header banners.

If you haven't installed Sourcerer, see the *Installing Sourcerer* recipe in *Chapter 7, Extending Joomla! and VirtueMart*.

 You do not need to follow the *Installing jQuery with Sourcerer* recipe because it is not necessary to complete this recipe. In fact if you have completed the *Installing jQuery with Sourcerer* recipe, then you should disable that module before continuing here.

Most modern websites have a cool feature or two. One popular feature with all types of website including e-commerce is a sliding header. See `www.hadronwebdesign.com` for an example of what I mean.

The nice thing about sliding headers is that as long as the picture looks good and the slider well implemented, it will enhance the whole site. You can prepare the images with messages like special offers or featured products. Then whenever there is something new to highlight in your store; just make a new image, upload, and replace an old one.

The good news keeps coming. There are many free sliders in the Joomla! extension folder. It is true that an easily installable Joomla! extension would be a bit simpler than this recipe to install. But the bulk of the work which is preparing the images still has to be done.

The advantage of doing things the way we will see in this recipe is that you are not tied to just what is available in the Joomla! extensions folder. If you were to search for free jQuery slider, you will get a ton of genuine hits. One top result had over 80 headers to choose from on one site!

So by doing things this way, you have infinitely more choices and the vast majority is free. This is very useful when you are making a site for a client because you can give them so much more choice.

I have chosen a really cool but straightforward fade-in/out jQuery plugin from `http://responsive-slides.viljamis.com/`. It is published under the MIT license so you can do most things with it for free. You can get the full unaltered code with loads of different samples direct from the aforementioned URL.

> I already mentioned that the advantage of doing things this way is the vast array of choices and different effects that are easily achieved for free. Even this single plug-in can be modified and configured in so many ways that I can't possibly mention them all here. I definitely recommend downloading the full package and experimenting. If you are wondering why I chose this particular option it is because it is responsive to different screen sizes and that's useful in this mobile age and for when we come to make our website in to an Android app later in the book. It is also a tiny file size which is great for the mobile world also.

I recommend that if you are new to jQuery/JavaScript or using them in a Joomla! context, you can copy the code from this recipe or download it from the Packt Publishing website.

Getting ready

Before we begin, prepare three nice images to use as your slides. Mine are 800 pixels wide and 250 pixels high. Yours don't have to be the same size as mine I suggest you experiment with different sizes and images to see what works best for you.

> I will be showing you how to put the code into the top featured article so the code appears directly below the header on the home page. But you could just as easily include the code directly in the header itself or even in the description box of a VirtueMart category or product to showcase some aspect of your product range etc. Just as long as the code is wrapped in the {source}{/source} tags Sourcerer/jQuery will do the rest.

Next, unless you love typing, download the folder containing all the code and files that you need from the Packt Publishing website.

How to do it...

1. Name your images `1.jpg`, `2.jpg`, and `3.jpg` respectively or modify the blank slides provided for your convenience in the download from the Packt Publishing website.

2. Upload them to the `images` folder in the root of your Joomla! install folder.

3. From the folder you downloaded, upload the following files, `responsiveslides.min.js` and `responsiveslides.css` to the root of your Joomla! install folder. These are the files provided by `http://responsive-slides.viljamis.com/` and contain the clever jQuery/JavaScript and the responsive screen size CSS.

4. In order to create banners in an article, from the Joomla! admin panel select **Content | Article Manager | New Article**.

5. Enter `Cool header` in the **Title** field as shown in the following screenshot:

6. In the **Category** drop-down box choose **Featured** to make the article appear on the home page as shown in the following screenshot:

7. Now type the following code or copy and paste it from the `source_to_paste.txt` file to the **Article Text** box:

```
{source}

  <link rel="stylesheet" href="responsiveslides.css">
  <script
src="http://ajax.googleapis.com/ajax/libs/jquery/1.8.3/jque
ry.min.js"></script>

  <script src="responsiveslides.min.js"></script>
  <script>
    // You can also use "$(window).load(function() {"
    $(function () {

      // Slideshow 1
      $("#slider1").responsiveSlides({
        maxwidth: 2000,
        speed: 800
      });
```

```
      });
    </script>

  <!-- Slideshow 1 -->
    <ul class="rslides" id="slider1">
      <li><img src="images/1.jpg" alt=""></li>
      <li><img src="images/2.jpg" alt=""></li>
      <li><img src="images/3.jpg" alt=""></li>
    </ul>

  {/source}
```

The following screenshot is a glimpse of the **Article Text** box:

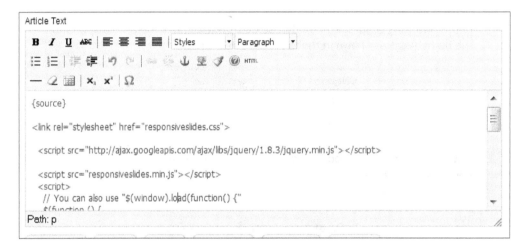

From the list of drop-down options on the right-hand side of the screen navigate to **Article Options** | **Show Title** | **Hide**.

We examine how the code works in the *How it works...* section next. Click on **Save and Close** and then read on.

1. Now we will make the article look like a proper banner by removing extraneous information as shown in the following screenshot:

2. Select **Menus** | **Main Menu** and then click on **Home**.

Depending on your configuration your home menu item might be called something different or be on a different menu. If so select it and read on.

3. From the list of drop-down options on the right-hand side of the screen, configure the following options as stated.

4. Navigate and configure **Article Options** | **Show Category** | **Hide**.

5. Navigate and configure **Article Options** | **Show Author** | **Hide**.

6. Navigate and configure **Article Options** | **Show Publish Date** | **Hide**.

7. Navigate and configure **Article Options** | **Show Hits** | **Hide**.

8. Navigate and configure **Article Options** | **Show Icons** | **Hide**.

9. Navigate and configure **Page Display Options** | **Show Page Heading** | **No**.

10. Click on **Save and Exit** and have a look at your home page.

How it works...

We uploaded the cool code that makes the whole thing work and configures the slider from `http://responsive-slides.viljamis.com/`.

The code we pasted into the article is surrounded by the `{source}{/source}` tags, thus the Sourcerer prevents it from simply being displayed as a normal article and the code is executed like it were a part of the Joomla! source files.

Here is a high level explanation of the code which should help you to quickly install other variations of it should you wish to.

```
{source}

  //The Soucerer start point

  //The code to load the simple but neat responsive CSS file we
  // uploaded earlier.
  <link rel="stylesheet" href="responsiveslides.css">

  //The code to load the jQuery library, this time from Google.
  <script
src="http://ajax.googleapis.com/ajax/libs/jquery/1.8.3/jquery.min.
js"></script>

  //The code to load the banner code we uploaded earlier and to
  //initiate jQuery.
```

```
<script src="responsiveslides.min.js"></script>
<script>
  // You can also use "$(window).load(function() {"
  $(function () {

//Load the specific piece of code from the main slider code. This will
//be one area to change when experimenting with other options.
// Slideshow 1
      $("#slider1").responsiveSlides({
        maxwidth: 2000,
        speed: 800
      });...

//The HTML formatted images to be manipulated. This section too would
//change when customizing.
<!-- Slideshow 1 -->
    <ul class="rslides" id="slider1">
      <li><img src="images/1.jpg" alt=""></li>
      <li><img src="images/2.jpg" alt=""></li>
      <li><img src="images/3.jpg" alt=""></li>
    </ul>

//The Sourcerer end point.
{/source}
```

The following screenshot shows how it looks on your desktop:

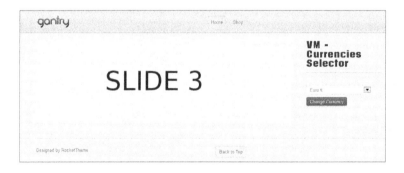

On a mobile phone, the slider is shrunk to the appropriate width, the menu links are converted to a mobile-friendly style and the **VM - Currencies Selector** module is popped neatly underneath, instead of to the side as shown in the following screenshot:

5
Going Live

In this chapter we will cover:

- ▸ Taking payments with PayPal
- ▸ Reset VirtueMart to a fresh install
- ▸ Configuring countries
- ▸ Configuring VirtueMart currencies
- ▸ Updating VirtueMart
- ▸ Creating a backup of your Joomla! VirtueMart site
- ▸ Using the backup of your Joomla! VirtueMart site
- ▸ Enable SSL for sensitive areas
- ▸ Shipping an order
- ▸ Refunding an order

Introduction

In this chapter we will do everything else that is necessary to make your store ready to present to real customers. For example connecting to a payment gateway.

In addition we will have a dry run at managing orders, refunds, and dispatch notices so that you know exactly what to do when the orders start rolling in.

Taking payments with PayPal

PayPal is the next most reliable payment system for taking payments directly on your website. By reliable, in this context I am talking about the likelihood of success of the transaction. That is, when the customer will actually part with their money.

PayPal allows customers to make payment without creating a PayPal account (most of the time) and also offers them the option of paying with their PayPal account should they want to.

PayPal are known for their overly generous stance towards the purchaser against the retailer, and if you are using PayPal you should make sure you obtain verifiable proof of posting and delivery for every order, or be prepared to have the order refunded. In addition be ready for complaints from customers who are occasionally forced into a PayPal sign up process. And they are infamous for occasionally freezing accounts without specific explanation. Always empty your PayPal account either daily or when you have accrued the minimum free withdrawal amount.

Getting ready

Sign up for a PayPal account if you don't have one already.

How to do it...

This is so easy that should make it harder just to make it more satisfying. In about 5 minutes we will be wired up to take our customers money.

1. Log in to your Joomla! site and go to your VirtueMart admin area. Click on **Shop | Payment methods**.

2. Now click on the **New** button in the top right. We are faced with two tabs. First up, the **Payment Information** tab. The page will look like the following screenshot:

3. From top to bottom, here is what we need to do. In the **Payment Name** field enter the title of the payment as it will appear to your customers. PayPal would suffice but based on customer preconceptions it could be beneficial to call it something like credit or debit card via PayPal.

4. Select **Yes** in the **Published** field.

5. In **Payment Description** we have an opportunity to give some more details to our customers to help them choose this payment option or not. Some might argue that this is the correct place to explain the Credit via PayPal issue, but that is significant enough to be in the title. In description, put whatever is useful to your customers. For the example used here it is, Choose this option to pay securely with your credit card on the PayPal website. You will also be given the option to use your PayPal account if you choose this option.

6. In the **Payment Method** dropdown choose **Paypal** as shown in the following screenshot:

7. Now click on **Save** and click on the **Configuration** tab.

8. Enter your PayPal e-mail address in the **PayPal payment email** field.

9. Click on **Save** and we are done.

   Now we need to tell PayPal where to communicate with your store so it can let you know that an order has been paid or not. VirtueMart can then update its records. The URL on your site that does this is: `http://www.yourwebsite.com/index.php?option=com_virtuemart&view=pluginresponse&task=pluginresponsereceived`

   Where `yourwebsite.com` is your actual domain name.

10. Log in to your PayPal account and select **Profile | My Selling Preferences | Instant Payment Notifications (Update) | Choose IPN Settings**.

11. Copy and paste the URL just discussed into the **Notification URL** box.

12. Select **Receive IPN messages** (enabled).

13. Click on the **Save** button.

How it works...

First we added PayPal as an option and configured it to be self-explanatory to your customers, and then we told PayPal to expect payments from your website and explained how to communicate with it.

Reset VirtueMart to a fresh install

If you have been following along with some recipes and experimenting to find the best options for you, then you might have some advantage of starting again from scratch. But having said that you might not want to go through the process of reinstalling Joomla! and reconfiguring what you have already done there.

I often end up doing this when I have a client who wants something a bit different that I haven't done before. I hack around getting stuff to work and finding the right solutions. Once I know and have documented exactly how to do something, I then reset VirtueMart so that I can implement things from a clean start.

 This process is irreversible. If you have spent time entering loads of products, custom fields, and so on, then this is probably not the recipe for you. This recipe will destroy VirtueMart and everything in it, then reinstall it how it was when it was first installed.

How to do it...

So you have definitely decided you want to turn the clock back to a completely fresh install. The following steps explain what you have to do:

1. VirtueMart hides away a little sort of virtual safety catch. So if you stumble upon the self-destruct button, that we will soon be using, and press it in a wild moment of thoughtlessness it won't work. So to flip the safety to off, click on the **Configuration** link from the **Configuration** menu in VirtueMart then click on the **Shop** tab.

2. Scroll down to near the bottom until you see the **Advanced Settings** area as shown in the following screenshot:

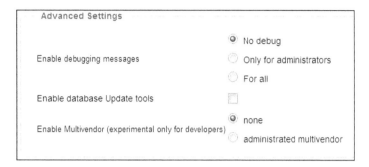

3. Check the box to the right of the label **Enable database Update tools** as shown in the following screenshot:

4. Click on **Save**.

5. Now select **Tools and Migration** from the **Tools** menu. Scroll down to the following big ominous looking buttons:

6. In a moment we are going to click on **Reset all tables and do a fresh install**. Consider one more time if this is the correct course of action for you.

7. Count backwards from 3 to 1 say blast off then click on **Reset all tables and do a fresh install**.

How it works...

First we flipped the safety to off, then we did a reinstall of VirtueMart. The database was wiped, the tables deleted, and VirtueMart reinstalled. Your former shop is gone. As the tables were reset to how they were, the safety catch is back on again automatically.

See also

▸ The *Creating a backup of your Joomla! VirtueMart site* recipe

▸ The *Using the Backup of your Joomla! VirtueMart site* recipe

Configuring countries

By default every country is available. By available we mean that a customer creating a new account can select it when filling in their address as shown in the following screenshot:

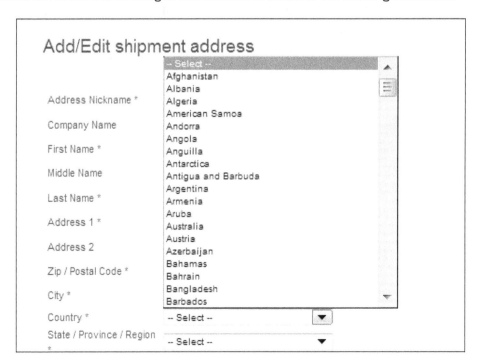

This is probably not what you want. There are likely many countries where you do not want shoppers to register from. For example, when based in Europe/USA, registering customers from Iran is unlikely to yield any benefit at the time of writing and many other more sensible reasons like the high cost of shipping to certain countries.

Removing countries is nice and easy.

Getting ready

Plan where you do want customers to register from and make a list in alphabetical order.

How to do it...

This is really easy and will only require five steps as follows:

1. In the VirtueMart control panel select the **Countries** link from the **Configuration** menu. You will see the list of countries available in VirtueMart.

2. Clearly there are hundreds of countries. VirtueMart spreads them over loads of pages. This can be cumbersome to manage. So at the very bottom of the page in the **Display** drop down, select **400** as shown in the following screenshot:

3. This should then make all the countries visible on one very long page. At the very top of the page select the checkbox above the first country as shown in the following screenshot. This will select every country.

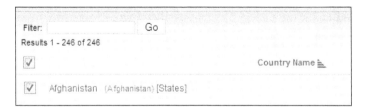

4. Now click on **Unpublish**.

5. In alphabetical order scroll down the list checking the boxes of the countries you do want to accept registrations from. Then click on **Publish**.

How it works...

De-selecting every country makes it simple to add back the countries we want to accept registrations from. Of course, if you wanted to accept registrations from more countries than you didn't want to, you could have left them all checked then gone through unchecking the ones you do want and then clicking on **Unpublish**. But that is slightly counterintuitive, so we did it the other way.

See also

▸　The *Configuring VirtueMart currencies* recipe

Configuring VirtueMart currencies

Offering multiple currencies makes the customer feel like you are making an effort to cater for them. It also makes browsing and assessing value much easier for them. There are no technical challenges for us, VirtueMart takes care of the conversion to match the correct price and PayPal will pay you in your native currency as usual.

Getting ready

Make a list of all the currencies you want to accept. You might like to briefly look at the *Removing the currency not defined error* recipe from *Chapter 1, Setting Up Shop*.

How to do it...

If you need to add more currencies than the one default currency that we configured in *Chapter 1, Setting Up Shop*, then the following steps explain how to do it.

1. Select **Currencies** from the **Configuration** menu.
2. From the **Display** drop down box choose **400**. This will make all the currencies visible on one page and make things easier for us as shown in the following screenshot:

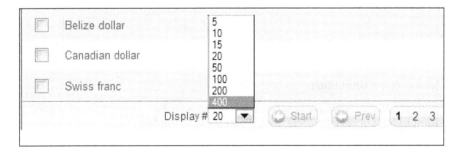

3. Select the top selection box to select all the currencies as shown in the following screenshot:

4. Click on **Unpublish**.
5. Individually select all the currencies you want to accept.
6. Click on **Publish**.
7. Now we have published the currency. We need to add them to our list of accepted currencies. On the main VirtueMart side menus select the **Shop** menu and then the **Shop** link. Now click on the **Vendor** tab (if you are not on it already).
8. Click on the **List of accepted currencies** field in the **Currency** box and choose **Select All Options**. Your store now accepts all your published currencies.

How it works...

By unpublishing all the currencies first, we won't accidentally accept any rogue currencies (unless we need to).

We then individually select the currencies we do want to accept. The following is the currency dropdown or the store front:

 Notice that VirtueMart kindly works out the conversion rate for us.

Updating VirtueMart

VirtueMart are fairly good at releasing updates, security patches, and improvements. It is always a good idea to keep up to date for the reasons just implied.

If you see the following screenshot on the left hand side of your VirtueMart control panel, then it means there is a newer version of VirtueMart available. Don't click on it just yet, we need to prepare first.

Getting ready

VirtueMart and Joomla! updates are extremely reliable. I have never "broken" a website by updating Joomla! or VirtueMart. But if you have custom coding, custom template files, extensions which might or might not be compatible, or perhaps are just a bit unlucky; you could trash your entire site by clicking on the update button.

So consider what other extensions you have, check with the provider if they will be compatible/might need upgrading as well and continue.

It is an essential good practice to always have a very recent backup at hand and when you intend to embark on something like a VirtueMart update, it is a good time to bring that backup kicking and screaming up to the current day. So if you need a hand with your backup, skip ahead and read the *Creating a backup of your Joomla! VirtueMart site* recipe. You could also consider cloning the site to a sub domain and test the update there first.

 Disregarding the preceding paragraph could result in a very bad day!

How to do it...

If you have done the research then the rest of this will work perfectly. The following steps explain what we will do:

1. So you have a working backup. We can now quickly update VirtueMart. Click on the big **Update Found** button shown previously.

2. Read the Updates and Improvements section, as shown in the following screenshot, there will often be neat new features or improvements that are otherwise not immediately obvious.

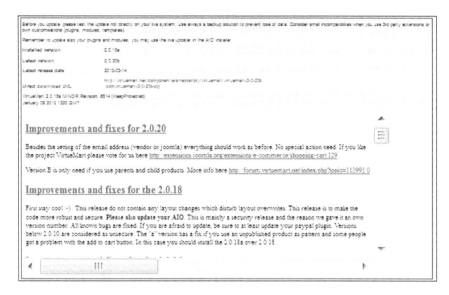

3. Click on the **Update to the latest version** button as shown in the following screenshot:

4. There is a message for us reminding us to update our VirtueMart modules as shown in the following screenshot. So click on the **Go to the Shop** button.

5. Check that the file, the button leads us to is the same version number that we just updated VirtueMart to. Download the new AIO to your desktop. The page will look like the following screenshot:

6. Now we will install the download. In your Joomla! admin area select **Extensions | Extension Manager**.

7. In the **Upload Package File** area click on the **Browse** button and choose the file you just downloaded ending in **_aio.tar** as shown in the following screenshot:

8. Now click on **Upload and Install**. If all has gone well you will see the following message:

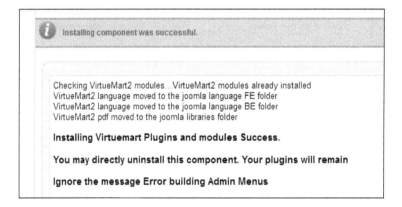

9. So let's do that now. To uninstall the AIO package simply click on the **Manage** tab, type `allinone` in the **Filter** box, click on **Search**, put a check mark next to the item to be removed and click on the uninstall (bin shaped) button in the row of buttons as shown in the following screenshot:

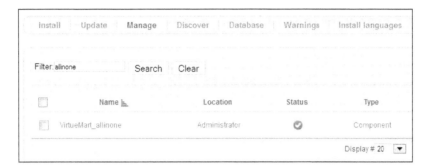

And we are done.

How it works...

Updating VirtueMart is a breeze but it is always sensible to take precautions and make sure we can recover if something goes wrong. In addition a little bit of research into any extensions we are using that might be affected is always worthwhile. VirtueMart and its core components are now up to date.

There's more...

In the unlikely event that this all went horribly wrong for you and you are left without a properly functioning site then assuming you have a backup you can simply follow the recipe, *Using your Joomla! VirtueMart backup*. You will be back to where you were in around half an hour.

See also

▶ The *Creating a backup of your Joomla! VirtueMart site* recipe

Creating a backup of your Joomla! VirtueMart site

Making and testing a backup should be part of any web administrator's regular routine. There are so many things that can go wrong. Not least of which is getting hacked or having malicious code implanted on your site.

Imagine if while checking your sites appearance in Google results you click on the link to your site and are faced with the following screenshot:

This is not good. It might be possible to remove the offending files but how do you know for sure that all is well. The best way is to wind the clock back to a happier time by wiping your site and using a backup.

As well as with nasty people messing with your site, it is not hard for an accident to occur. If you are using custom code that accesses the database then it only takes one wrong table to be deleted or even just altered in the wrong way and yours or your clients income is gone.

Getting ready

Let's make a backup of your site so that we can rest easy. How often you should back up your site depends upon how frequently it is changing. For example, if I am working on a new unlisted site perhaps on a development URL we will back up at the end of each day. Some might even consider this a bit too laid back. After all losing a days work is a big deal and as we will see it only takes 20 minutes to do a backup.

If you run a site which receives orders every day (and you will soon) it is worth backing up at least daily. Explaining to a day's worth of customers that you have their money but no idea what they ordered is awkward enough. More than that is downright irresponsible and it will guarantee you lose some repeat customers, not to mention the immense inconvenience and loss of time sorting things out.

Another issue is testing your backup. The best way to do this is to run a testing server. You can then make your daily (or whatever) back up and then immediately deploy it to your testing server. Setting up a testing server is not covered in this book but is not tough and is well documented online.

Start by searching for WAMP. WAMP is a nicely packaged and easily deployed server environment that is also free. When you have a WAMP environment you can then practise deploying your backups using the next recipe, *Using your Joomla! VirtueMart backup*.

How to do it...

Let's get our site backed up and put on a disc in the cupboard. The first thing to do is to prevent any changes occurring to the files or database during the backup process. We will take the site temporarily offline.

1. From the main Joomla! drop down menu select **Site | Global Configuration**.

2. Click on the radio button for **Site Offline**, click on the radio button for **Use Custom Message**, and in the **Custom Message** text box write a short explanation of what is occurring so as not to lose any customers. The page will look like the following screenshot:

3. Now click on the **Save** button.

Now the first major part of the back up is to make a copy of the database. Some web hosts will have easy to use database backup tools but so we can all follow along. We will copy our database using PHPMyAdmin. A pretty much standard tool for performing functions with a MySQL database.

1. Log in to your web hosts control panel and look for something like the following screenshot:

2. Click on **phpMyAdmin** and log in by entering your database username and password. If you have forgotten them then you can find them by reading the `configuration.php` file in the root folder of your Joomla! installation.

3. Click on the name of your database and then you should see a long list of all the tables. We need to select all the tables. Depending on which setup of **phpMyAdmin** you have, this could be at the top or the bottom of the list. Find it and click on **Check all** or **Select all**.

4. When all the tables are selected/checked as shown in the following screenshot click on the **Export** button.

5. Just make sure the options shown in the following screenshot are checked:

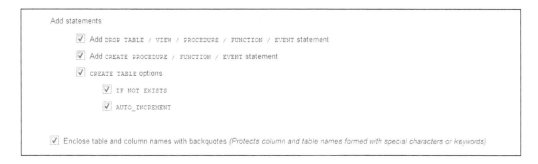

6. It will now delete and recreate all the tables in the process but leave the actual database setup intact. This is especially useful in hosting environments where you do not get to choose the name of your database. The one option to check is that the output of the export process is going to be to a file. Click on the **Save output to a file** option if necessary as shown in the following screenshot:

7. Click on **Go**. Retrieve the downloaded file from the usual place you retrieve downloads from your web browser, and place it on your desktop. The file will have the `.sql` extension.

    Next we will make a copy of all the files that Joomla! and VirtueMart use to access the database and display our website to the world.

    Some web hosts will have a handy utility in your web control panel for this. You might have the option to make a compressed copy of a folder for example, and then download the compressed file.

8. We will do it in a way that can be easily duplicated regardless of the web host that you use. Open FileZilla. If you haven't downloaded and set up FTP access with FileZilla you can find out how in the *Installing Joomla! 2.5 in your web space* recipe in *Chapter 1, Setting Up Shop*.

9. Connect to your site by selecting **File | Site Manager | Your Site | Connect**. In the right hand window of FileZilla, browse so that you can see the files that are not actually within your main Joomla! folder. Mine is called **joomla25**, you can see it in the following screenshot in the right hand FileZilla window.

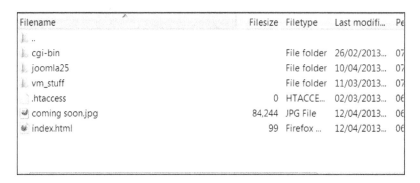

10. Here on the right hand side of the FileZilla window you can see where we have selected **Desktop**, (as shown in the top of the following screenshot) and the current contents of my desktop (as shown in the bottom window of the following screenshot) where I am about to add the folders I want to copy/back up.

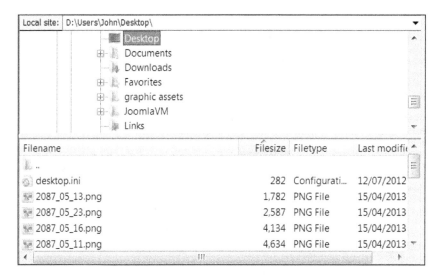

11. Now we clearly need to copy our main Joomla! folder, in this case **joomla25**. But we also need to copy the folder pointed to by our VirtueMart safe path. In this case `vm_stuff`.

If the VirtueMart safe path is news for you then take a look at the _Fixing the safe path_ recipe in _Chapter 1, Setting Up Shop._

12. Now select the two folders we need to copy (in the case of this example **joomla25** and **vm_stuff**) from the right hand window and drag them both across to the desktop window on the left. The download might take some time.

13. Put them on a disk as well as a pc not anywhere on the web server, obviously.

14. Put your site back online by selecting **Site** | **Global Configuration** and checking the **Site Offline** | **No** option from your Joomla! admin panel.

15. Put the disc away somewhere safe to avoid it being used as a coffee coaster.

How it works...

Now we have a copy of everything we need to completely reconstruct our Joomla! site from nothing.

See also

▸ The _Using the backup of your Joomla! VirtueMart site_ recipe

Using the backup of your Joomla! VirtueMart site

So disaster has struck! Here is how to get things up and running again and try and avoid future disasters.

Getting ready

We will assume a typical scenario. Files are infected/deleted and the database is corrupted beyond repair. It could actually be a little bit worse. The database could have been deleted. In which case you would need to recreate it using your web hosts database tools as you would have done in the _Installing Joomla! 2.5 in your web space_ recipe in _Chapter 1, Setting Up Shop._

How to do it...

Put the files you created while doing your site backup from the *Creating a backup of your Joomla VirtueMart site* recipe, on your desktop.

1. Open FileZilla and connect to your site. File | Site Manager | Your site | Connect.

2. Let's start clean. In the right hand window of FileZilla, right click on your corrupted Joomla! install folder and select **Delete** as shown in the following screenshot:

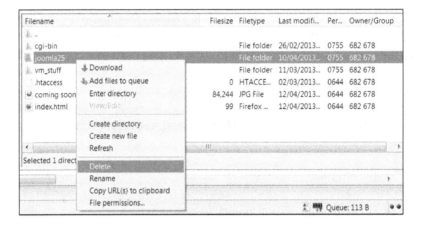

3. Next, when FileZilla is ready, delete the VirtueMart safe path folder, in this case it is **vm_stuff**. Right click and click on **Delete**.

4. Now, in the left FileZilla window navigate to your desktop as shown in the following screenshot:

5. Drag the previously backed up uninfected and tested VirtueMart safe path folder and the main Joomla! install folder over to the same position as there recently deleted versions. Wait for the process to complete.

6. Log in to your web hosts control panel and look for something like the following screenshot:

7. Click on **phpMyAdmin** and log in by entering your database username and password. If you have forgotten them then you can find them by reading the **configuration.php** file in the root folder of your Joomla! installation.

8. Click on the name of your database. Now click on **Import** and then **Browse**. Find and select the database file ending .sql, that was created during the backup recipe as shown in the following screenshot:

Find the **Go** button and click on it. You should be able to log in to your site again. The following screenshot displays the page after the import is successful:

Import has been successfully finished, 327 queries executed. (bvdcdmru_joomla25.sql)

After restoring your site it is well worth trying to work out how it happened in the first place. Now would be a good time to consider your sites security measures in general. Especially and perhaps most urgently changing the login to every aspect of your website.

9. Change the login to your Joomla! store by logging in and selecting **Users | User Manager | Super User**. Enter a new password in the **Password** and **Confirm Password** fields as shown in the following screenshot:

Password	
Confirm Password	

 You might consider changing your username as well and making the password longer and containing more hard to guess characters like non alphanumeric.

10. Change the login to your database via your web hosts control panel. Now you have locked Joomla! store out of the database and it will not function. Using FileZilla find the file configuration.php in the root Joomla! install folder. Find this entry, the one that starts with **public $password = '...'** as shown in the following screenshot:

```
public $host = 'localhost';
public $user = '          ';
public $password = '            ';
public $db = '            ';
public $dbprefix = '       ';
```

11. Change it to match your new database password. Be sure to leave the surrounding quotation marks and ending semicolon in place. Upload it to the root Joomla! install folder from where it came.

12. Change the login to your web hosts control panel.

13. Change the login to your site FTP.

14. Log in to your Joomla! admin panel. From the main Joomla! drop down menus select **Site | Global Configuration**.

15. Check the radio button for **Site Offline (no)**.

16. Now click on the **Save** button.

How it works...

We basically rewind time to the point of our most recent backup. The degree of usefulness of this process and the amount of inconvenience experienced by yourself and your customers will be directly related the amount of time that has elapsed since you did the last backup.

So back up regularly and test your backup!

See also

▶   The *Creating a backup of your Joomla! VirtueMart site* recipe

Enabling SSL for sensitive areas

This is so easy but so important. It is possible to snoop in on communications over the Internet. So what about, when your customers are typing sensitive data into your site?

In reality this is more about protecting your sales than customer data. Nowadays customers are quite sophisticated and if they don't see a reassuring padlock icon or notice that the address is http instead of https when filling out forms, they will probably quit and buy elsewhere.

SSL will ensure that the private information the customers share with you, will be encrypted during transit.

Getting ready

Order an SSL certificate from your hosting provider by buying it from their website or giving them a call. It shouldn't cost more than $50 a year and you can often get discounts by committing to multiple years.

How to do it...

Once you have confirmation from your web hosts that the SSL certificate is active then we can proceed.

1.   From your VirtueMart control panel select **Configuration | Configuration**. Then on the **Shop** tab scroll down to the following screenshot:

> Enable SSL for sensitive areas (recommended) ☑

2.   heck the **Enable SSL for sensitive areas(recommended)** option.

3.   Click on **Save**. We are done here.

Once your hosting provider has done the technical stuff and set up an SSL certificate for your domain you can just flip the switch to encrypt the relevant areas of VirtueMart.

Shipping an order

I remember my first e-commerce order many years ago. It was an extremely liberating moment. When I realised that maybe, just maybe I could make a living at this thing. Then it dawned on me that I had no idea what to do next and liberation was replaced with dread.

Getting ready

Get your shop ready to sell with great product descriptions and a fantastic template. Now go ahead and wait for somebody to buy something. If nobody buys anything see the following tip.

If there is no customer yet then *Chapter 6, Killer SEO* could help. If not, phone a friend ask them to buy something and refund it in the next recipe.

How to do it...

So you have got somebody to place an order, either a friend or a real customer. When you receive an order VirtueMart will send you an e-mail as shown in the following screenshot:

[0af703], Order confirmed by Washupito's Tiendita, total 250,03 €

Joomla25   16/04/2013 1

To: John;

055555 Canangra	Spain
Spain	Santa Cruz de Tenerife
Santa Cruz de Tenerife	555-555-555
555-555-555	

SKU	Product Name	Product status	Price	Qty	Tax	Discount	Total
P02	Circular Saw Diameter 10	Confirmed by shopper	172,20 €	1	43,39 €	0,00 €	250,03 €
		Product prices result			43,39 €	0,00 €	250,03 €

1. From your VirtueMart control panel select **Orders and Shoppers | Orders**. You will see the new order in your control panel as shown in the following screenshot:

2. Before you do anything else check that the transaction was as successful as it appears, by logging into your payment provider, to check that the payment was actually made.

3. Now just click on the **order number** that you want to process. And then the **Update Status** link on the right of the screen, as shown in the following screenshot:

Now we can enter all the details and enter a new status into the pop up box as shown in the following screenshot:

4. Change the **Order Status** drop down to **Shipped**.

5. Write a friendly message to the customer telling them that their order is on the way.

6. Click on **Save**.

7. Actually wrap and ship the order. VirtueMart doesn't do that for us yet.

How it works...

When a customer buys something the order appears in your VirtueMart control panel. From there you can keep your customer informed and keep a record of what is occurring with the order.

See also

▶ The *Refunding an order* recipe

Refunding an order

Hopefully this will be a rare event. But it is bound to happen to even the best product range in the world. It is usually best to give in graciously and process things promptly. Here is what to do.

Getting ready

To complete this recipe we first need a customer to buy something and then request a refund. You could get a friend to make a purchase and then refund it as a practice run for when you get the first real refund request.

How to do it...

So we have our first grumpy customer and the only way to appsease them is to give them their money back. The following steps explain what to do:

1. From your VirtueMart control panel select **Orders and Shoppers | Orders**.

2. Now just click on the **order number** that you want to refund. And then the **Update Status** link on the right of the screen.

3. Change the **Order Status** drop down to **Refunded**.

4. Write a friendly message to the customer telling them their money is on the way back to them.

5. Click on **Save**.

6. Actually log in to your payment provider and check whether the order has been refunded.

How it works...

Quite simply, with a few clicks we have returned the customers money and updated the status of the order.

See also

▸   The *Handling an order* recipe

6
Killer SEO

In this chapter we will cover the following topics:

- ▸ Installing Piwik analytics
- ▸ Setting up Piwik for Joomla!
- ▸ Setting up Piwik for VirtueMart
- ▸ Choosing your keywords
- ▸ Creating categories in Joomla!
- ▸ Creating articles in Joomla!
- ▸ Making your articles available in a menu
- ▸ Enabling Joomla! SEF URLs
- ▸ Understanding and writing great metadata
- ▸ Entering your metadata into Joomla!
- ▸ Entering your metadata into VirtueMart

Introduction

SEO or search engine optimization could easily fill its own book. So in this chapter we will concentrate on just one aspect of SEO. On-Page SEO refers to the actual work/optimization we do on the website itself.

Before we implement a SEO campaign we need a way to track our site's performance.

We will now effortlessly set up one of the best open source analytics software – Piwik analytics. Piwik analytics is stuffed full of benefits over and above the likes of Google analytics. You can learn more about this in the first recipe, *Installing Piwik analytics*.

After our analytics is up and running, we will go through the process of implementing the most vital aspects of On-Page SEO; everything from choosing our keywords to writing articles and metadata.

Installing Piwik analytics

Piwik is stuffed full of so many features, that it would easily take a small book to explain. But it is so simple to use once it is setup.

From your drag-and-drop control panel you can see live data on your site as well as all the usual metrics such as visitors, keywords that they used, products they purchased, and the conversion rates.

In addition to this, you can keep all your own data. Piwik runs on your server, hence you know that certain big global dominant providers aren't using your own data for commercial gain or even against you.

If you are a web developer, your customers will love Piwik analytics. Offer it to them as a deal sweetener. It can even be easily re-branded from within the Piwik control panel. The following figure shows three partial screenshots with details such as page view history, product sales history, and e-commerce revenue:

The following figure has three partial screenshots showing a color-coded visitors report, real-time visualization of where in the world your visitors are from, and a report showing the number of visits per page:

Many of the features of Piwik are too detailed to go into in this varied chapter but once they are setup, it is extremely easy to log in, explore, and analyze.

 You can even monitor your site's performance via Piwik with the help of this cool and free Android App, available at `https://play.google.com/store/apps/details?id=org.piwik.mobile&hl=en`.

If you want all these Piwik features, read on.

Getting ready

Head over to `piwik.org` and click on **Download** menu and then click on the nice big **Download Piwik 1.xx.x** button to get the latest version. When you have the zip file named `latest.zip`, we will look at installing it.

How to do it...

This process is fairly long but each step is nice and simple when taken on its own. In brief, we first put the files on the web server, then we create a database for Piwik to use and finally we install Piwik by running the installer.

So let's get started. Perform the following steps to begin with the installation:

1. Use FileZilla create a folder in your root web folder called `analytics`. Note this is the same level as the Joomla! install folder if you followed the *Installing Joomla! 2.5 in your web space* recipe in *Chapter 1, Setting Up Shop*. The reason we do this is because Piwik can handle the analytics of multiple websites. Shortly afterwards, when you get to the actual installation of Piwik you will need to access this folder via an URL in your browser. This URL will usually be the default domain name for your hosting account.

 You could, for the sake of tidiness create and point a sub-domain, perhaps called `analytics.yourdomain.com` to point to the `analytics` folder. But this is not essential.

2. Unzip the file `latest.zip` to your desktop.

3. Switch FileZilla to binary mode by selecting **Transfer | Transfer Type | Binary** from the top FileZilla menu.

4. Using FileZilla, upload the entire unzipped `piwik` folder to the recently created `analytics` folder on your web server or upload and unzip using your preferred method.

5. Now, in order to set up a new database, log in to your web hosting control panel and create a new MySQL database. When you have done so, there will most likely be a database details screen where you can grab the details that are ready for the installation of your Piwik analytics. Make a note of your database name, username, password, and hostname.

6. Now visit the URL `http://yourdomain.com/analytics/piwik` or just type your sub-domain `analytics.yourdomain.com/piwik` if you set it up alternatively as mentioned in the previous tip. The following screenshot shows the opening screen of the Piwik analytics setup:

7. There is no work required in the previous screenshot. Just click **Next** to proceed.

8. At the top of the next screen you will see the **System check** heading. If all is well there should be green ticks for each item. Review and contact your web host wherever necessary such as any item that do not have a neat little tick next to them as shown in the following screenshot:

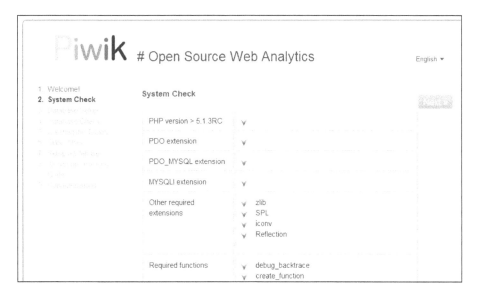

9. Scroll down to the section with the heading **Optional**. Any red crosses here might not be an essential thing to fix but read the Piwik comments next to any red crosses and take the recommended actions. An example of a recommendation is shown in the following screenshot:

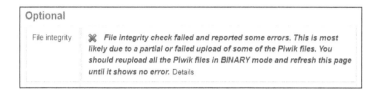

Optional instruction in case of optional error—after switching FileZilla to binary mode by selecting **Transfer | Transfer Type | Binary** from the top FileZilla menu (if you haven't already), uploading the page again, and finally refreshing the page in your browser by pressing *F5* on your keyboard, you will be all good to go.

The following screenshot is shown after the recommendation is accepted:

10. Click on **Next** and we see the **Database setup** screen as shown in the following screenshot:

11. Copy and paste the details you recorded in the fifth step. All the fields are often self-explanatory and match to what they will be called in your web hosting control panel but there are some exceptions to this. The one labeled **database server** refers to the database location and will sometimes be called **Hostname** on shared hosting. So you might need to delete the default **127.0.0.1** and replace it with your **Hostname**. In addition to this, **login** might be referred to as **Username** in some web hosting setups.

12. Leave the **table prefix** as the default **piwik_** this will allow you to install other applications on the same database should you need to at a later date.

13. When you have entered all your details, click on **Next**. Now we are getting somewhere. We can now see the following screenshot:

14. Click on **Next** again.

15. This screen might look like trouble but it is simply asking you to choose your Piwik login details. Choose a user name and type it in **super user login**, a nice and secure password into **password** and **password (repeat)** and your e-mail address into **email**. I suggest we leave the last two options checked so we receive informative and sometimes important security alerts from Piwik as shown in the following screenshot:

16. Click on **Next** again.

17. Enter your website name, URL, time zone (where you are) in the appropriate fields, and most importantly in the bottom dropdown labeled **Ecommerce,** select **Ecommerce enabled**. You can see the one already configured as shown in the following screenshot:

18. Click on **Next** (yet again).

19. The next screen is the **Tracking code** screen. We are going to do things a little differently. We are going to install tracking for Joomla! and VirtueMart areas of our site and we are going to install advanced e-commerce tracking options (this is much easier than it sounds). So we just need to skip this screen by clicking on, you guessed it, **Next**.

How it works...

We did it. We got the Piwik files, put them on the web server, installed them, and now we can log in to our Piwik analytics center. Just visit the URL you installed Piwik to. Either `http://yourdomainname.com/analytics/piwik` or `analytics.yourdomainname.com` as shown in the following screenshot:

You can now log in to Piwik and explore.

▸ The *Setting up Piwik for Joomla!* recipe

▸ The *Setting up Piwik for VirtueMart* recipe

Setting up Piwik for Joomla!

Before you follow this recipe you should have completed the previous recipe *Installing Piwik analytics*. Piwik analytics tracks as many websites as you like. This recipe simply enables it on a specific Joomla! website. Repeat this recipe for every site you wish to track.

Getting ready

Visit `http://www.nfrtest.de/en/downloads-en/category/1-plugins`. Choose the appropriate download for your version of Joomla!. This guide, like most in this book is using Joomla! 2.5.x, so we download the file `nfrpiwik251.zip`. Keep it on your desktop and get started.

How to do it...

Setting up Piwik for Joomla! was nice and quick. now we can start gathering data in our Piwik database.

1. Log in to your Joomla! control panel and select **Extensions | Extension Manager**. Find the area with the label **Upload package file** as shown in the following screenshot:

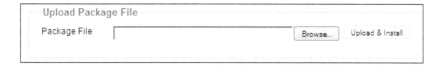

2. Click on **Browse** and find the `nfrpiwik251.zip` file on your desktop. Select it and then click on **Upload and install**.

3. Now from the main Joomla! menu select **Extensions | Plug-in Manager**. Find the search box as shown in the following screenshot:

4. Type `piwik` and click on **Search**. We can now see the Piwik plugin clearly listed as shown in the following screenshot:

5. Just put a tick in the check box next to **Piwik**, like in the previous screenshot and then click on **Enable** from the main row of buttons at the top of the screen.

6. Now let us install the tracking code. Leave this browser page open, we will come back here in a minute. Open a new browser page or a tab. Go to your Piwik analytics control panel and log in.

7. In the top right-hand corner click on the **Settings** link. It is next to the **Sign out** link as shown in the following screenshot:

8. Look at the menu of links on the left-hand side. Click on the **Tracking Code** link as shown in the following screenshot:

9. Scroll down the page and find the section labeled **Javascript tracking code**. Click on the code to highlight it, press *Ctrl + C* to copy it.

10. Go back to your web browser tab/window with the **Plug-in Manager** page already open. Click on the plugin link **Piwik** to open the plugin configuration page, then navigate to **Basic Options | Tracking code** as shown in the following screenshot:

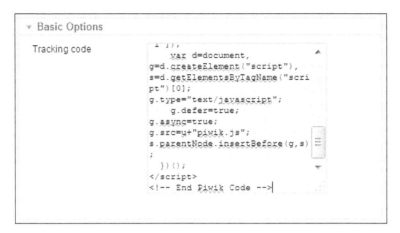

11. Paste the code you just copied. To paste the code, press *Ctrl + V* on your keyboard.

12. Finally click on **Save**.

That's it.

How it works...

What this recipe actually did was to put the tracking code into the Joomla! files in just the right place. It is not actually changing the functions of our Joomla! site in any way. We could have copied and pasted the code directly into the `index.php` file but that would have been prone to over-writing during Joomla! updates, not to mention that if you mess with the Joomla! core files unnecessarily, then we can cause problems such as breaking the site.

We then pasted our personalized Piwik tracking code to let the data gathering commence.

See also

▶ The *Setting up Piwik for VirtueMart* recipe

Setting up Piwik for VirtueMart

Here we will set up the advanced e-commerce features. This will allow us to look at data like cart contents and abandonment, revenue tracking, sales, and perhaps the most interesting, conversion rate.

Getting ready

The download for the required plugin can be obtained from `http://extensions.virtuemart.net/statistics/piwik-for-virtuemart2-detail`. Put the zip file on your desktop and read on. The rather easily forgettable filename is `plgvm_istraxx_vmpiwik_vm2.0.12_1.0.zip` with the numbers on the end varying if the version has changed since this was written.

How to do it...

Now we have the necessary file on our desktop, so let's set them up in VirtueMart as shown in the following steps:

1. Log in to your Joomla! control panel and select **Extensions | Extension Manager**.
2. In the **Upload Package File** area click on **Browse**.
3. Choose the `plgvm_istraxx_vmpiwik_vm2.0.12_1.0.zip` file from your desktop and then click on **Upload and Install**.
4. Now navigate to **Extensions | Plug-in Manager** from the main Joomla! menu.
5. In the search box type `virtuemart piwik` and click on **Search**. We can now clearly see the VirtueMart Piwik plugin as shown in the following screenshot:

6. Put a tick in the check box next to the plugin labeled **System - VirtueMart 2 Piwik** as shown in the previous screenshot and click on **Enable** from the main row of buttons on this page. Now click on the **System - VirtueMart 2** link itself to open up the configuration page.
7. Everything can be left as the default except **Piwik URL** which needs to have the URL of your Piwik installation in it. If you followed the *Installing Piwik Analytics* recipe, then this will either be the domain name that points to the root of your public HTML area or if you used the tip given in that recipe it will be at the sub-domain suggested. So for the former enter `yourmaindomain.com/analytics/piwik` or the latter enter `analytics.yourmaindomain.com`.
8. Click on **Save** and we are done.

How it works...

The VirtueMart Piwik plugin communicates with our Piwik installation to gather really useful statistics and information that can help us optimize our website.

Choosing your keywords

Most of the rest of the recipes in this chapter talk about entering metadata, writing meta descriptions, writing articles containing your keywords, and so on. But which keywords should you optimize your website to perform for?

The short answer is to choose the same words your customers will use to find the information or products you are selling. But they will be many and varied. This recipe will help you decide and get you started on finding the absolute best keywords for your business.

Getting ready

Before you start, you need to consider your strategy. Do/will you have a vast site that has hundreds of articles and thousands of products? If you do then the task ahead is vast too. You will need to focus on one category of products or articles at a time when you work through this recipe.

If your range of products and articles is more niche, then that might save you a fair bit of time when it comes to keyword research but it makes the decisions around *which* keywords to optimize harder.

Whichever situation you fit into, a good place to start is your key market and the most generic keywords. We have used the example of a company selling cakes made without eggs in their ingredients.

To complete this recipe we will be using the Google keyword tool which can be found in your Google Adwords control panel. If you don't have an Adwords account you can sign up for one on http://www.google.co.uk/ads/adwords/get-started.html.

To complete this recipe you will also need to grab a free copy of OpenOffice from http://www.openoffice.org/download/.

You need this to export the data that we create during the mai part of the recipe.

How to do it...

Searching for the best keywords is an iterative process. When you follow this quick recipe using your own keywords, opportunities will probably present themselves at different times to our cake-specific flavored example. Perform the following steps:

1. Decide on the scope of this search (site, category, sub category article category, and so on) and think of the one word that sums up the scope of this research Let's choose **Cake**. Enter it in Notepad or any other text editor.

2. On a new line in the text editor write a two or three word key phrase, the most generic you can think of to describe the scope of this research. Let's choose **egg free cake**.

3. Log in to your Google Adwords account.

4. Find the keyword tool by navigating to **Tools and Analysis | Keyword tool**.

5. Copy and paste your keywords from your text editor into the keyword tool area labeled **Word or phrase** as shown in the following screenshot:

6. Now click on **Search**.

7. At the top of the search results are two tabs. Click on the **Keyword ideas** tab and you can see a whole load of keyword ideas including the two you started with near the top. Notice there are probably multiple pages of them as shown in the following screenshot:

8. At the top of the list click on **Global Monthly Searches**. This will sort the results with the most popular searches first.

9. Now in our list there are 800 results. Here is how to refine them. Scroll through the lists and click through the pages to find the first (and therefore most popular) highly relevant key phrase. Don't just pick something generic. For example I am researching "egg free cakes" so I will ignore all the phrases at the top of the list, they are just about "cakes" not "egg free cakes".

10. When you have found the most popular, highly relevant phrase type it into the **Word or phrase** box with your other two phrases. You may find "eggless cakes" after three pages of searching. Click on **Search** again.

11. Repeat steps 9 and 10 a couple of times more.

12. Now click on **Save All** from the top of the list of generated keywords and **Save All** from the top of the list of the keywords you entered and navigate to **Download | My Keyword ideas** as shown in the following screenshot:

13. In the next box, choose **CSV**. Confirm the download.

14. Open the file in OpenOffice Calc. We can sort the data to make it easy to find the best keywords as shown in the following screenshot:

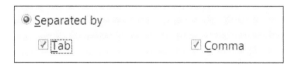

15. When you are presented with the previous options, tick the boxes marked **Tab** and **Comma** as shown in the previous screenshot.

16. Now click on **OK** and we will do some sorting.

Notice that the exported data is of a slightly different format than how it appears in the keyword tool. The **popularity** column which is used to classify things as **high** or **low** has numerical values ranging from **0** to **1**. **0** means there is no competition for advertising, **1** is very strong competition, and everything else is degrees in between. By competition we mean paid competition for Google Adwords.

Hopefully you came across some words or phrases that are quite numerous and some words or phrases that are very high volume. Add to this, you might have come across these words or phrases in a context unrelated to your products. I found that "eggless cake" was a popular term. So pick your first term to explore and we will sort to view the data more clearly.

17. In OpenOffice select **Data** | **Sort**.

18. Select the options **Global Monthly Searches** and **Descending** as shown in the following screenshot:

19. Now we want to filter by our first term to explore and order it by popularity. The term is "eggless cake". Follow along swapping out "eggless cake" for your term.

20. Select **Data** | **Filter** | **Standard Filter** as shown in the following screenshot:

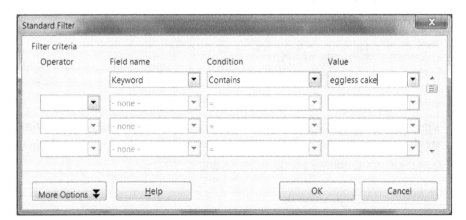

21. Fill out the filter criteria options as follows and as shown in the previous screenshot by navigating to **Field Name | Keyword, Condition | Contains** and **Value | eggless** cake (insert your term here). Click on **OK**.

22. Now you can see the top volume searches for eggless cakes. You can see some of the findings in the *How it works...* section after this recipe.

 Create your own tables of data and screenshot all your top tens. Make a presentation in a word processor document and make notes about opportunities you spot. You will begin to amass a really good understanding for your industry. This tip is particularly useful if you need to present an SEO solution to a client.

23. Repeat steps 19 to 22 for all the phrases/keywords that interest you. If you find an interesting keyword without many variations, go back to step 10 to expand your dataset. Don't forget to filter your starting key phrase as well.

24. Complete this process in short bursts of maybe half an hour. As your knowledge of the opportunities around the words that interest you grows, you will think of many more words and phrases to add in step 10. And, other ways to filter from step 20. If the process takes less than a week you either have a very small niche or you have missed loads of opportunities.

25. If you have a wide industry to investigate, repeat this process from step 1 for every category and subcategory. Probably using a great find from the initial process to start your second process.

How it works...

Here they are, just some of the opportunities uncovered in the first 20 minutes of searching. I show you them not because there is much chance you are interested in eggless cake but to point out the opportunities that can arise from this process.

Keyword	Opportunity
Eggless cakes	Totally new high volume, low competition alternative to egg free cakes
Recipes for eggless cake	Perfect heading for a Joomla! category of tasty recipes.
Cake without egg	Another phrase totally different but almost as high search volume as my initial starting point. This can be used in conjunction with either eggless or 'egg free and still sound perfectly natural.
Why eat eggless cake	Search volumes up there with recipes. Perfect for an article
Egg free/Eggless cupcakes	The most popular cake without eggs by a factor of three. Even more than chocolate or cream!

Iteration, sorting, filtering, and presenting helps our brains make sense of the mass of data that even the tiniest niche will have. We now have a good selection of keywords and phrases to use in our product descriptions, categories, and site articles.

Creating categories in Joomla!

Writing a regular blog, tutorials, or topical articles related to the products and industry around those products can generate lots of visitors to your website. Planning, as with most things in SEO is probably as important as the actual articles themselves.

Having devised the most appropriate keywords for your site, you are probably half way there on deciding the categories you should divide your articles into. Logical divisions make the customer more likely to see a category that interests them and click to investigate.

If you have lots of articles, then subcategories might be worthwhile as well. In this recipe we will create three categories. One will also have three subcategories within it.

Getting ready

Plan your article category structure carefully. Think about the keywords and the long tail keywords from the *Choosing your keywords* recipe. The longer the keyword, the deeper it should be put in the structure. With the absolute best keyword (for your strategy) and longest being in the articles themselves.

With this in mind and using a completely abstract scenario this recipe will create the following categories and subcategories. During the recipe, simply switch out the abstract category names for your real category names and alter the structure to suit you.

The following screenshot shows how our category structure looks like after implementation in Joomla!:

How to do it...

Let's get started by logging in to the Joomla! control panel. Perform the following steps:

1. From the main Joomla! menu, select **Content | Category Manager | Add New Category**.

2. Enter the title of the first category in the **Title** field. We enter `Category 1` in our example.

3. The next and only other necessary box to complete is the **Description** box. Click on the box to enter a description.

4. The description can be as long or short as you think is appropriate. The category description will appear above the list of articles in the category when a visitor clicks on it to view the category. Notice that you can format your category description just like you can if you were using a word processor. Be sure to use the appropriate keywords in your category description.

5. Click on **Save & Close**. Now you can see your newly created category in the categories list as shown in the following screenshot:

6. Click on **New** and repeat steps 2 - 5 for each of the top level categories. Now we have three categories in the list as shown in the following screenshot:

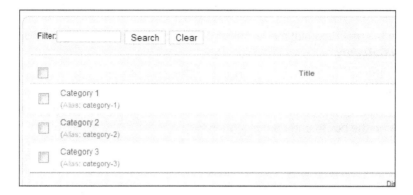

7. Now for the subcategories nested inside **Category 2**. Specifically, **Subcategory 2a**, **Subcategory 2b**, **Subcategory 2c**. Click on **New** as usual, enter the name and description for your first subcategory in the normal way.

8. Now find the drop-down box labeled **Parent**. Click on it and choose which category to place this subcategory into. In the given example, **Category 2** as shown in the following screenshot:

9. Click on **Save & Exit**.

10. Repeat steps 7 - 10 for all your subcategories. You can see we now have an arrangement of categories and subcategories just as we intended.

Technically speaking Joomla! doesn't have subcategories which they call them parent and child categories. There used to be just sections and categories but this arrangement was inflexible. Now you can have multiple layers of categories, subcategories, sub subcategories, and beyond but using the parent and child structure we have seen here.

How it works...

By setting up an easy to use (for our customers) category structure we can now add some actual articles to give customers and the search engines that tell them about us, more reasons to visit.

The following is a screenshot of the completed category structure:

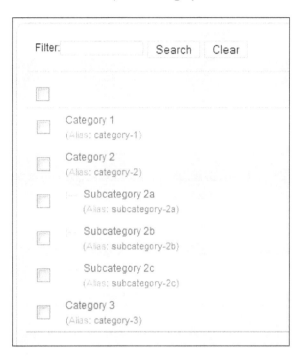

See also

▸ The *Creating articles in Joomla!* recipe

Creating articles in Joomla!

Here we will add some articles to the categories we created in the *Creating categories in Joomla!* recipe. Think back to your keyword research in the recipe Choosing your keywords. Often the title of an article that could be really popular will present itself in that research.

Getting ready

First of all you need to write your article. Remember to include the words, short and long tail that the article is being optimized for.

How to do it...

So you have your articles to hand or some great ideas ready to tap out into Joomla! Let's get them published as shown in the following steps:

1. From the main drop down Joomla! menus select **Content | Article Manager | Add New Article**.

2. Enter the title of your article in the **Title** field as shown in the following screenshot:

3. In the drop-down list labeled **Category**, select the category that this article should go in to as shown in the following screenshot:

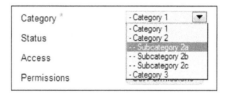

4. In the section labeled **Article text**, write or copy and paste the actual article excluding the main heading of the article which we entered in the **Title** field previously as shown in the following screenshot:

5. Format your article to make it easy to read and scan. Don't forget to use a generous but natural selection of the keywords you are targeting in the headings, paragraphs, and where relevant bold, underline, and links. This is easy using the formatting buttons at the top of the **Article text** area. And be sure to complete the image and text if you add any images to your article as shown in the following screenshot:

6. Now click on **Save & Close**.
7. Repeat all the previous steps to publish all your articles.

How it works...

By entering articles that our visitors will find interesting and contain the words which they are using to search for the information contained within those articles, we are helping the search engines to help our future readers to find us. When they arrive on our site and see what great articles and products we have for them, we can turn them into customers.

See also

▸ The *Making articles available in a menu* recipe

Making articles available in a menu

If you have followed the last few recipes you will have an effective category structure and some really interesting articles in them. So the search engines start sending people to your articles and your readers like them and want more. We need a way for them to browse our article categories.

Getting ready

This is a really quick and simple recipe which will place a category menu in the top left side of the standard Joomla! template on every page.

How to do it...

This will only take a minute. If you are not using the default Joomla! template, the only variation to this recipe will be choosing a different position name to put your menu where you want it.

1. In order to create the menu, from your Joomla! control panel select **Menus | Menu Manager | Add New Menu** as shown in the following screenshot:

2. All we need to do here is enter a title for our menu of categories in the field labeled **Title**. Copy and paste the same words into the **Menu Type** field as well. Then click on **Save & Close**.

3. In order to create the top level (parent) category links (items) in our menu, click on the menu you just created. The example here was the somewhat unimaginative **My Categories** as shown in the following screenshot:

4. Now we can start to add the menu items for each of our categories. We will start with our top level (parent) categories. Then go back and do the sub (child) categories. Click on **New**. We can now see the **New Menu Item** screen.

5. The following screen is not as daunting as it might first appear. Here is what to do. Click on **Select** to the right of the **Menu Item Type** label as shown in the following screenshot:

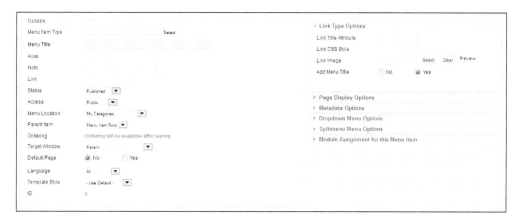

6. Now we have to choose a page type that this menu item will link to. Experiment with the different types but a good one to show visitors what we have on offer is **Category Blog**. This will show a short snippet of the latest articles from the category that we will choose soon. Choose **Category Blog** by clicking on it now.

7. Notice the rest of the options on the page have changed slightly to reflect our last choice. Most notable and helpful, to the top right of the screen in the **Required Settings** section is a drop-down list labeled **Choose a category**. Click on the drop-down list and you will see that we can now assign this menu item to any category we want. For the sake of logic, pick the first of your categories. In this example it is **Category 1** as shown in the following screenshot:

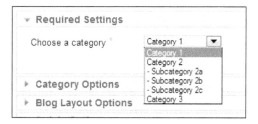

8. One more thing to configure for this menu item is the actual text of the link. Enter a short, appropriate, self-explanatory, and SEO-friendly text into the box labeled **Menu Title**. This text may well be as simple as the category name. But whatever makes sense to do on your site as shown in the following screenshot:

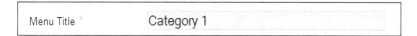

9. Click on **Save & Close**.

10. Repeat steps 3 - 10 linking to a new category each time, until all the top level (parent) categories have been created.

11. To create a subcategory, click on **New** as usual.

12. Select the **Menu Item Type** exactly as before. Be sure to choose a sub category in the **Choose a category** drop-down list and as before, type a title (the text for the link) in the **Menu Title box**.

13. Now we do things slightly differently. Look down the options of the main **Details** block on the left-hand side of the screen until you find the **Parent Item** option as shown in the following screenshot:

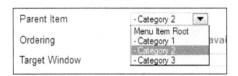

14. As shown in the previous screenshot, choose the parent of this sub (child) category.

15. Click on **Save & Close**.

16. Repeat steps 11-15, choosing a different subcategory and choosing the appropriate parent each time. In the following screenshot, you can see our menu laid out exactly to match the categories we created two recipes back:

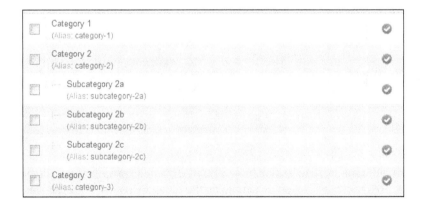

17. So now we have our menu configured, it is time to display it on our site and instantly make all our categories, subcategories. and articles available to the world. Navigate to **Extensions | Module Manager | New**.

18. From the **Select A Module Type** list choose **Menu**.

19. In the **Menu Title** field type, type My Categories or something appropriate as a title for your menu.

20. Next to the **Position** label, click **Select Position**. For the default template choose **position -7** to position our new menu on the top left. This choice will vary from template to template.

21. On the right side of the screen in the **Basic Options** section, click on the drop-down list next to the **Select Menu** label. Choose the **My Categories** option or whatever you called your new menu as shown in the following screenshot:

22. Almost done. Set the option **Show sub menu items** to **Yes**.

23. Click on **Save & Exit**.

How it works...

Using the Joomla! menu and module systems we quickly made a menu of all clickable links available to each of our categories. We then positioned our new module with our menu in it, on our site. Click on some of the links and check out the category blog format that we chose as shown in the following screenshot:

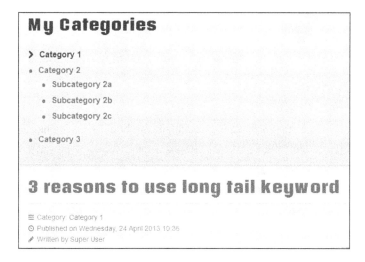

Enabling Joomla! SEF URLs

Search Engine Friendly (SEF) URLs are an effective way of improving the experience that customers have on your website at the same time as fine tuning the results that a search engine might generate. Add to the good news that it is a simple one minute job to set them up and it makes sense to enable them.

Have a look at the following two URLs:

- Without SEF URLS

  Consider the link `yourdomainname.co.uk/index.php?option=com_content &view=category&layout=blog&id=18&Itemid=162` just as an example. These type of links are not so good because they have none of our keywords and it is confusing to read them.

- With SEF URLS

  The link `yourdomainname.co.uk/index.php/category-1/28-3-reasons-to-use-long-tail-keyword` is good enough, as we can read the keywords.

- In VirtueMart

  And lastly we have the link in the form `yourdomainname/shop/powertools/ outdoortools/chain-saw-detail`. You can see how they are not only friendly to the search engines but also help your site be more intuitive to our human visitors.

More good news is that VirtueMart 2 uses SEF URLs by default so when we click on the right button in Joomla! and then everything else will take care of itself.

Getting ready

Log in to Joomla! and get ready for the fastest, neatest bit of SEO you ever did.

How to do it...

This is possibly the quickest *How to do it...* section in the book and yet one of the most beneficial. Perform the following steps:

1. Navigate to **Site | Global Configuration**.
2. Click on **Search Engine Friendly URLs** radio button to **Yes** as shown in the following screenshot:

3. Click on **Save & Close**.

How it works...

We have told Joomla! to use friendly URLs and now our customers see more intuitive representation of where they are on our site. Added to this, the search engines can be even more sure about what page that they are on is all about.

Writing great metadata

Ever looked at the source code of your Joomla!/VirtueMart site?

Apart from the potential information that the search engines can gather about the content on your website, it also has an effect on the likelihood or not of a potential visitor clicking on your link.

Getting ready

The following table provides a quick explanation of the types of metadata:

Type	How it appears in source	Explanation
description	`<meta name="description" content="our words here"/>`	This is almost certainly the most useful of all the metadata. Not only do all the major search engines read this to help assess the content of the page but often it will be used in their actual search results also.
keywords	`<meta name="keywords" content="keyword1, keyword 2 etc"/>`	Potentially this is the least important metadata. Some search engines specifically state that they do not use this field anymore. But it is an opportunity to specify exactly what this page is all about and it is a good practice to complete it.
title	`<meta name="title" content="..."/>`	This is what you see in the tab of the web browser. Joomla!/VirtueMart writes this for us from the article/product/category title. As we go through the recipe, after this one, however you will see the Title option and can override the default if you want to.

How to do it...

This recipe should act as a step-by-step checklist and guide you to write effective keyword lists and more importantly, meta descriptions. Our imaginary scenario is a cake shop whose biggest selling point is that their cakes do not contain any egg.

1. In order to write a meta description, open a text editor like Notepad for Windows.

2. Decide and reduce in size your site USP, preferably in maximum three words. In the example we have `Made without egg`.

3. Write the most vital piece of information about the page you are working on and include the most specific and appropriate long tail keyword. Perhaps put a cool adjective in there as well. Do so in one brief sentence. Here we typed `Buy delicious Black Forest Gateaux`.

4. Now add your site USP that applies to your business at the end of the site. What makes you different. In the example, we have added **Made without egg!**.

5. If it is appropriate to your business situation, add your company phone number, if it will be significant or useful to the searcher. If you add this extra information keep the rest of the sentence brief. If you don't want/need to use a phone number you have a bit more artistic license with the rest of your description.

6. Now, lets have a look at call to action. Good examples include "click for more", "visit us now", and so on. The one used in the example is, `Get your egg free cake today!`.

7. Now we put all the parts together in one snippet like `Buy delicious Black Forest Gateaux - Made without egg! -Tel:12345678910. Get your egg free cake today!`.

8. Now count the number of characters.

9. If the characters are less than 160, you probably could add a little more information. This is because 160 is the number of characters that Google will show as a snippet in the search results. If you are refining it further, make sure to leave it in each of the vital sections. In our example, there are just over 100, so I will add a bit more, `Buy delicious Black Forest Gateaux from the best cake shop in UK NoEggCake.com - Made without egg! -Tel:12345678910. Get your egg free cake today!`.

 If you have reached this stage and you are still not happy with your meta description then why not have a look at how your competitor does it? In Firefox, visit the page whose meta description you want to learn from. Then press and hold the *Ctrl* key and tap *U* on the keyboard. Start a search by pressing *Ctrl + F*. Now type `description` and press *Enter* on the keyboard. The first occurrence is likely to be the meta description you are looking for. Here is what I found following this tip on the Packt Publishing home page:

```
<meta name="description" content="Packt Publishing provides
books, eBooks, video tutorials, and articles for IT developers,
administrators, and users." />
```

1. Writing the meta keywords is much easier. Scan the page from the top left to the bottom right. Type every keyword or key phrase that occurs anywhere on the page. So as an example the text, "Egg free Black Forest Gateaux" would yield the list, **Egg, Egg free, Black Forest Gateaux, Egg free Black Forest Gateaux**.

2. Delete any keyword or phrase that you have entered more than once.

How it works...

We are now prepared to produce some great quality meta descriptions and some accurate keyword lists. Use this method when completing the next two recipes.

Entering your metadata into Joomla!

You may wonder what is entering metadata into Joomla! all about or if you have not prepared metadata, please take a look at the *Writing great metadata* recipe. When you're ready to go, read on.

Getting ready

The biggest mistake that clients make with regard to metadata is that they use site wide metadata. Joomla! even has a box where you can enter site wide meta descriptions and keywords.

The key to having highly effective metadata is to specifically tailor it to each and every page. It will then have precisely the right keywords for every article. Google will notice the continuity and your search rank for the page might improve because of it.

But even more important than this is your future readers/customers will see your meta description in the search engine results page and it will be a finely tuned introduction with a call to action to click and get the full information.

So as you go from article to article, entering your metadata, do not be tempted to speed things up by copy-pasting duplicates. Follow the *Writing great metadata* recipe very specifically in the context of each page.

How to do it...

The hard part is writing the metadata, but Joomla! makes it really easy to enter. Here is what to do:

1. To enter the site wide metadata, select **Site | Global Configuration** from the main Joomla! menu. Scroll down a bit and you will see the following screenshot:

2. Enter your handcrafted, specific, meta description in the **Site Meta Description** field and your entire keyword list that covers the whole site in the **Site Meta Keywords** field.

3. Click on **Save & Close**.

4. In order to select categories, navigate to **Content | Category Manager**.

5. Click on the article to add metadata to. On the right hand side click **Metadata Options**.

6. Enter your handcrafted, specific, meta description in the **Meta Description** field and your keyword list specific for that whole category and only that whole category in the **Meta Keywords** field.

7. Click on **Save & Close**.

8. Repeat steps 5 - 7 for each of your categories. Don't forget all the sub (child) categories.

9. To edit article, select **Content | Article Manager**.

10. Click on your first article to edit it.

11. On the right-hand side of the page but you might need to scroll down a little, click on **Metadata Options** and you will see the following screenshot:

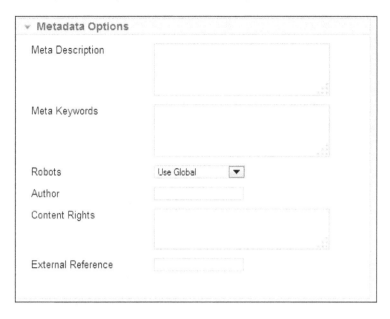

12. It is just the first two boxes we are concerned with. Enter your handcrafted, specific meta description in the **Meta Description** field and your keyword list specific for that whole article and only that whole article in the **Meta Keywords** field.

13. Click on **Save & Close**.

14. Repeat steps 10 - 13 for all your articles.

15. In order to refine your metadata, wait for your meta descriptions to turn up in the search engine results pages. (you might like to go and do something else in the mean time as this can take between 5 minutes and some weeks.) When they are there look to see if they are truncated at the end as they might need shortening a character or two.

How it works...

By entering your hand crafted metadata into the convenient boxes provided by Joomla! in the category and article pages, you are confirming the precise and specific content of your pages to the search engines and giving an enticing reason to your clients to come and visit you.

See also

▸ The *Entering your metadata into VirtueMart* recipe

Entering your metadata into VirtueMart

You may wonder what is entering metadata into VirtueMart all about or if you have not prepared metadata please take a look at the *Writing great metadata* recipe When your ready to go read on.

Getting ready

At the risk of repeating myself if you have completed the *Entering your metadata in Joomla!* recipe, the key to having a highly effective metadata is to specifically tailor it to each and every product as well as each product category.

Each page crawled by Google will then have precisely the right metadata to match the contents. Google will notice the continuity and your search rank for the page might improve because of it.

But even more than this is people searching for your products or range will see your meta description in the search engine results page and it will be a finely tuned introduction with a call to action to find the product/range they are looking for.

So as you go from product-to-product and category-to-category entering your metadata, do not be tempted to speed up the process by copy-pasting duplicates. Follow the *Writing great metadata* recipe very specifically in the context of each product/category.

How to do it...

Once we know how to write the metadata, the rest is easy. So let's get it done.

1. From the VirtueMart control panel select **Products | Categories**.
2. Click on the category to add metadata to it. Scroll down to near the bottom and here you can see the area that interests us as shown in the following screenshot:

3. We need to enter our unique meta description, specially crafted for this category only in the **Meta Description** box and the keywords relevant to only this category in the **Meta Keywords** box.

4. Click on **Save & Close**.

5. Repeat steps 2-4 for all the categories and subcategories.

6. From the left hand VirtueMart menu select **Products | Products**.

7. Click on the product to add meta tags to it. Next, select the **Product Description** tab. Scroll down until you find the following screenshot:

8. We need to enter our unique meta description, specially crafted for this product only in the **Product Meta Description** box and the keywords relevant to only this product in the **Product Meta Key** box. Ofcourse this box should have been labeled **Product Meta Keywords** but there is a typing error in VirtueMart.

9. Click on **Save & Close**.

10. Repeat steps 7-9 for each of your products.

11. Wait for your meta descriptions to turn up in the search engine results pages (you might like to go and do something else in the mean time as this can take between five minutes and some weeks). When they are there, look to see if they are truncated at the end as they might need shortening by a character or two.

How it works...

By entering product or category specific metadata into the convenient boxes provided by VirtueMart you are sending a message about the content of your product pages to the search engines and giving an enticing reason to your clients to come and visit you.

See also

▸   The *Entering your metadata in Joomla!* recipe

7
Extending Joomla! and VirtueMart

In this chapter we will cover:

- ▶ Installing Sourcerer
- ▶ Installing jQuery on Joomla! 2.5 using Sourcerer
- ▶ Personalizing your store content with Sourcerer
- ▶ Detecting the user's country with Sourcerer and GeoIP
- ▶ Installing Weever Apps
- ▶ Configuring a Weever App
- ▶ Installing the VM Affiliate component
- ▶ Setting up a campaign and then testing it with VM Affiliate

Introduction

This chapter is all about the things that Joomla! and VirtueMart can't do on their own but with the help of a friendly extension can quite simply and usually for free, be extended to do.

We look at Sourcerer for messing with JavaScript, jQuery, and PHP, then the really cool but sadly not free VM Affiliate for getting an affiliate campaign working in a span of about half an hour. Also for turning your site content into something that resembles an app we look at Weever App.

Installing Sourcerer

Sourcerer is one of the most versatile Joomla! extensions. It allows you to add custom code (HTML, JavaScript, or PHP) at almost any point in Joomla!. This facilitates everything from custom database calls with output, to jQuery visual tricks. In this recipe we will take the first step by installing Sourcerer.

Getting ready

Download the free Version of Sourcerer from `http://www.nonumber.nl/extensions/ sourcerer`.

Put the downloaded file on your desktop and follow this brief guide to install it.

How to do it...

If you have the download ready then read on. We will simply install Sourcerer and will do some fancy things in later recipes.

1. From the Joomla! admin panel navigate to **Extensions | Extension Manager**. Click on the **Browse** button and select the file `sourcerer-v4.1.x.zip`. Now click on **upload and install**.

2. To check that Sourcerer is working we will create a custom module and try and use a bit of PHP. Navigate to **Extensions | Module Manager** and then click on the **New** button. At the end of this step you would see a screenshot like the following one:

Select a Module Type:	
Archived Articles	Articles Categories
Articles Category	Articles - Newsflash
Articles - Related Articles	Banners
Breadcrumbs	Custom HTML
Feed Display	Footer
Language Switcher	Latest News
Latest Users	Login
Menu	Most Read Content
Random Image	RokNavMenu
Search	Smart Search Module
Statistics	Syndication Feeds
VirtueMart Category	Virtuemart Currency Selector
VirtueMart Manufacturers	VirtueMart Products
VirtueMart Search Product	VirtueMart Shopping Cart
Weblinks	Who's Online
Wrapper	

3. Click on **Custom HTML**.

4. Now let's configure the module and try out some PHP. In the **Title** field enter `Sourcerer test`. And now click on the **Select Position** button.

5. Choose a prominent position, **position-7** is top-left on BEEZ or perhaps, **content-top-a** is a good one if you are using the Gantry framework.

6. Let's assign this module to every page by selecting **On all pages** on the **Module assignment** dropdown near the bottom of the page as shown in the following screenshot:

7. Finally the fun bit. In the custom output area enter the following code as shown in the following screenshot:

```
{source}
<?php
    echo 'Sourcerer is working!!!';
?>
{/source}
```

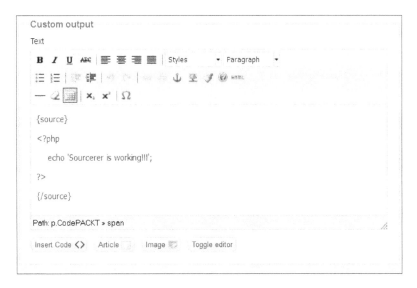

How it works...

We have installed Sourcerer and our little test should produce output similar to the following screenshot:

Sourcerer inserts your code in exactly the module you enter it. This makes custom programming that would otherwise be potentially complex, a breeze. Future recipes will do some slightly more practical things with Sourcerer.

See also...

> ▶ The *Installing jQuery on Joomla! 2.5 using Sourcerer* recipe

> ▶ The *Personalizing your store content with Sourcerer* recipe

> ▶ The *Detecting the user's country with Sourcerer and GeoIP* recipe

> ▶ The *Cool header banners with jQuery and Sourcerer* recipe, in *Chapter 4, Making Your Store Look Amazing*

Installing jQuery on Joomla! 2.5 using Sourcerer

Here we will use Sourcerer to let us do cool jQuery stuff from within a Joomla! module. jQuery is a JavaScript library which greatly simplifies and speeds up some of the exciting things that can be done with JavaScript. Being able to summon this magic directly from within Joomla! and VirtueMart can be extremely useful.

Getting ready

We will simply load up jQuery. Once jQuery is loaded you can use anything from the entire jQuery library, right within Joomla!.

How to do it...

This is nice and easy so let's get started.

1. To install the Google jQuery library, we will create a custom module and load it directly. Navigate to **Extensions | Module Manager** and then click on the **New** button. At the end of this step you would see a screenshot like the following one:

2. Click on **Custom HTML**.

3. Now let's configure the module and try out some PHP. In the **Title** field enter Sourcerer test. And now click on the **Select Position** button.

4. Choose **debug**.

5. Let's assign this module to every page by selecting **On all pages** from the **Module Assignment** dropdown near the bottom of the page as shown in the following screenshot:

6. Learning jQuery is beyond the scope of this book but it really doesn't matter as long as you can copy and paste, as this way all the recipes will work for you. Now we link to the jQuery library, load jQuery, and enter some really simple code to see if it worked. Enter the following code in the **Custom output** area as shown in the following screenshot:

```
{source}
  <script src="http://code.jquery.com/jquery-  latest.min.
js"type="text/javascript"></script>
  <script type="text/javascript">
  jQuery.noConflict();
  jQuery(document).ready(function() {
    jQuery("a").click(function() {
    alert("Hello world!");
    });
```

```
});
</script>
{/source}
```

7. Click on **Save** and we are done.

Downloading the example code

You can download the example code files for all Packt books you have purchased from your account at `http://www.PacktPub.com`. If you purchased this book elsewhere, you can visit `http://www.PacktPub.com/support and register` to have the files e-mailed directly to you.

How it works...

Apart from setting up jQuery, the code also tells the web browser to pop up an alert box whenever the user clicks on a link as shown in the following screenshot:

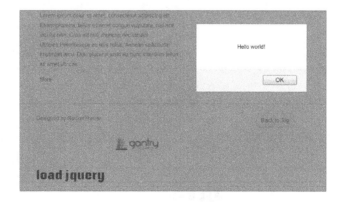

Now we have even more things that we can do with Sourcerer and jQuery.

See also...

- ▸ The *Installing Sourcerer* recipe
- ▸ The *Personalizing your store content with Sourcerer* recipe
- ▸ The *Detecting the user's country with Sourcerer and GeoIP* recipe
- ▸ The *Cool header banners with jQuery and Sourcerer* recipe, in *Chapter 4, Making Your Store Look Amazing*

Personalizing your store content with Sourcerer

There is no end of tricks you can perform with Sourcerer. Anything that can be done in PHP, JavaScript, HTML, or CSS can be neatly placed on any page at just about any place and without having to hack around with the Joomla! or VirtueMart code.

In this recipe we will see how easy it is to personalize a product description. That is, to use the customer's name as if speaking to them personally. It is a sales technique used by bricks and mortar stores and can make a difference to how your customer feels about you and your products.

Getting ready

Make sure you have Sourcerer installed. If you didn't follow the previous recipe *Installing Sourcerer* this will help you to set it up in just a few minutes.

How to do it...

Now let's add a personal greeting to the `Smaller shovel` product description. Of course there is a good chance you are not selling gardening equipment. This recipe can be easily adapted to work in any article, category, Joomla! HTML module, or product. Anywhere you can enter text, you can enter the Sourcerer tags and the enclosed code.

1. From the VirtueMart control panel select **Products | Products**.
2. Click on the product for which you want to add personalization to. In this case we click on **Smaller Shovel**.
3. Click on the **Description** tab and click on the **Product Description** editing area right before the normal product description.

4. Leave a couple of lines of space at the start of the **Product Description** area and enter this code as shown in the following screenshot:

```
{source}
<?php
    echo "Hi ". $user->username . " look at this great shovel!";
?>
{/source}
```

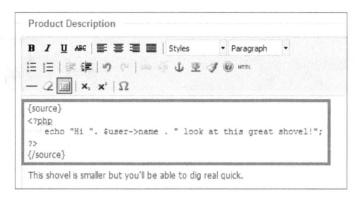

5. Click on **Save**.

How it works...

Now when we visit the product in our storefront while we are also logged in to Joomla!, we see something like the following screenshot:

Sourcerer makes available to us commonly used Joomla! objects and their member variables. So when we use this PHP code:

```
echo "Hi ". $user->username . " look at this great shovel!";
```

In between the Sourcerer tags:

```
{source}{/source}
```

And the regular PHP tags:

```
<?php
?>
```

We output a friendly message that will be customized to whichever user is logged in.

See also

▸ The *Installing Sourcerer* recipe

▸ The *Installing jQuery on Joomla! 2.5 using Sourcerer* recipe

▸ The *Detecting the user's country with Sourcerer and GeoIP* recipe

▸ The *Cool header banners with jQuery and Sourcerer* recipe, in *Chapter 4, Making Your Store Look Amazing*

Detecting the user's country with Sourcerer and GeoIP

What we will do is detect which country a visitor to our website is from and vary the content we show accordingly. In this simple recipe we will detect if a visitor is from UK, Spain, or Germany and output a message in the appropriate language. You will be able to easily adapt or extend the code should you wish to cater for more countries or different countries. This will work by using Sourcerer to query a GeoIP database which tells us where the current visitor's IP address is registered.

Getting ready

If you haven't installed Sourcerer then see the recipe, *Installing Sourcerer*, in this chapter.

Pick an article, product, category, or Joomla! HTML module in which to do this. We will be installing the code in an article but with Sourcerer, as always, it would be trivial to amend the recipe and put the code somewhere to suit you.

How to do it...

This can appear quite technical at times but it really isn't. Understanding the PHP is not essential either. So if the code makes you feel bad, just follow along step-by-step.

Getting the database and the API:

1. The database is not one that needs to be installed in the same way that the Joomla! database was. All we need to do is download the latest free Version of `Geoip.dat` and that is what we do now. Visit `http://dev.maxmind.com/geoip/legacy/geolite`.

2. Scroll down to the **Downloads** section. You might notice there is a legal obligation to attribute the `Maxmind` website when we use the free database. This is taken care of when we write our custom code.

3. Click on the **Download** link in the row labeled **GeoLite Country** in the **Binary / gzip** column as shown in the preceding screenshot.

4. Put it somewhere convenient like your desktop and extract it so you are left with a file `GeoIP.dat`.

5. Now we will get the API which is the PHP code that can get results from this database file. Visit `https://github.com/maxmind/geoip-api-php`.

6. Scroll down until you see **geoip.inc** as shown in the following screenshot:

7. Click on **geoip.inc**, and then near the top of the page find the **copy to clipboard** icon as shown in the following screenshot:

8. Click on the **copy to clipboard** icon. Paste the contents you just copied into your text editor and navigate to **File | Save as**. Name the file geoip.inc. Put the file somewhere handy like your desktop for the next step.

9. Using FileZilla, upload geoip.inc and GeoIP.dat to your Joomla! install folder. To be precise, inside the folder that contains the folders **Administrator**, **Cache**, and so on.

Install our code:

1. Create a new Joomla! article by navigating to **Content | Article Manager | New Article** from the main Joomla! menu.

2. Enter a name for your article in the **Title** field. I entered GeoIP.

3. Scroll down to the **Article Text** field and copy the following code or copy and paste from the code download section on the PACKT website. I have put comments in the code. The lines starting with // are to help you identify what is happening at each stage. (You can also refer to the screenshot following the code for this purpose.)

```php
{source}

<?php
  //Get the ip address of the visitor
  $ip=$_SERVER['REMOTE_ADDR'];

  //load the GEOIP code
  require_once JPATH_SITE.DS.'geoip.inc';

  //Open the GEOIP database file
  $gi = geoip_open("./GeoIP.dat",GEOIP_STANDARD);
```

```
//Get the visitors location and load it into $visitorslocation
//by cross matching his IP address with the geoip database
$visitorslocation = geoip_country_code_by_addr($gi, $ip);

//Close the database
geoip_close($gi);

//Print a mesage for visitors from spain
if($visitorslocation == "ES"){
  echo "Hola y cómo estás hoy";
}

//Print a mesage for visitors from Germany
if($visitorslocation == "DE"){
  echo "Hallo und wie geht es dir heute";
}

//Print a mesage for visitors from UK
if($visitorslocation == "GB"){
  echo "Hello and how are you today?";
}

?>

  <p>This product includes GeoLite data created by MaxMind,
available from
  <a href="http://www.maxmind.com">http://www.maxmind.com</a>.</p>
{/source}
```

4. Click on **Save**.

How it works...

Have a look at the article you just created, it will look something like the following screenshot when you are in the UK.

If in Spain, it looks like the following screenshot:

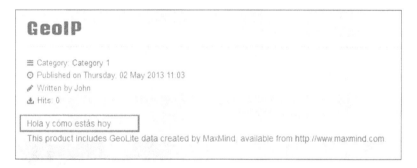

How it works is as follows:

- We put a free IP-Country code database on our web server.

- Then we put some free open source PHP code (an API) on our web server that knows how to use the database.

- Next, we added our own custom code that grabs the IP address of a visitor and uses the database via the free open source API code to tell us where the visitor is located. This went inside a regular Joomla! article wrapped in the Sourcerer {source}{/source} tags.

- We then vary our output accordingly. with the series of `if...` statements.

```
//Print a mesage for visitors from spain
  if($visitorslocation == "ES"){
    echo "Hola y cómo estás hoy";
  }
```

```
//Print a mesage for visitors from Germany
if($visitorslocation == "DE"){
  echo "Hallo und wie geht es dir heute";
}

//Print a mesage for visitors from UK
if($visitorslocation == "GB"){
  echo "Hello and how are you today?";
}
```

It is the country codes such as ES, GB, and DE that you need to change if you want to experiment with different countries.

And if you are wondering the budget for this book is big enough for a trip to Spain to take the previous screenshot then sadly it is not. I used the Firefox plugin `Geolocator` to spoof my geo-location. `https://addons.mozilla.org/en-us/firefox/addon/geolocater/`.

See also

- The *Installing Sourcerer* recipe
- The *Installing jQuery on Joomla! 2.5 using Sourcerer* recipe
- The *Personalizing your store content with Sourcerer* recipe
- The *Cool header banners with jQuery and Sourcerer* recipe, in *Chapter 4, Making Your Store Look Amazing*

Installing Weever Apps

I love Weever Apps. But they are not right for every situation. There are cheaper and potentially more advanced app options available. It all depends on your time budget and skill set available to you. In *Chapter 9, Blueprint – Making an Android App out of Your Site Content* we will be looking at one such alternative.

The benefit of Weever Apps is that they are just so easy to get your app up and working as we will see in the next recipe, *Configuring a Weever App*.

There are some less than obvious limitations however. For example, the website, `weeverapps.com`, makes an exciting statement about being compatible with all the major mobile operating systems. And technically speaking it is. But when you look in detail you need to pay $499 dollars for each app store submission.

So in reality the app is just an enhanced website. But it is a very convincing one. And the launch icon on your customers' device is actually a shortcut not an actual launch icon. But this is still potentially very effective marketing.

And even for Android apps, that have the bulk of the market share for smart phones and provide virtually free, virtually unrestricted submission for app developers, app store (Google Play) submission will not be possible without the hefty Weever charge because we don't have access to the native Android `.apk` file. Again, this is solved with a different solution in *Chapter 9, Blueprint – Making an Android App out of Your Site Content*.

However there is still enormous potential marketing benefit to deploying a Weever App and we can do it from start to finish in less than an hour.

Getting ready

Head over to `http://weeverapps.com` and have a look at the pricing and options. We will now set up the 15 day free trial so you can find out if this is for you.

How to do it...

Follow along and in around 10 minutes the Weever Apps component will be installed in your Joomla! setup.

1. Go to `www.weeverapps.com/pricing` and click on **Try for 15 days Free!**.

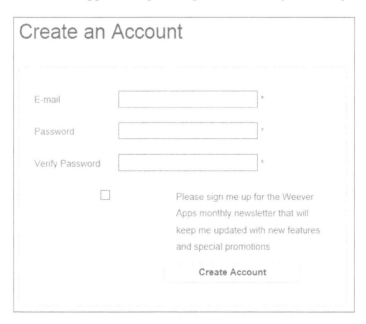

2. Fill out the brief **Create an Account** form and click on the **Create Account** button as shown in the preceding screenshot.

3. In the **Choose a Plan** section, click on **appBuilderTM for Joomla! or Wordclick on** as shown in the following screenshot:

4. In the part labeled **2.Enter your details** enter your website URL and be sure the radio button for **Free 15-day Trial of Pro** is selected as shown in the following screenshot:

5. Agree to the terms of service and click on the **Create New App** button.

6. Now we are on the Account manager screen. Click on the **Download** link highlighted in the following screenshot:

7. Click on the **Download 2.5 Component + Login Plugin** button. Confirm the download and place it somewhere handy like your desktop.

8. Now, from our Joomla! admin control panel we select **Extensions | Extension Manager**.

9. Click on the **Browse** button in the **Upload Package File** area, select the file we downloaded from `weeverapps.com`, mine is called `com_weever-all-J2.5-v1.8.2.1.zip`. Click on the **Upload and Install** button.

10. You will see various messages about the install progress. Don't close this browser tab.

11. In a different browser tab go back to `weeverapps.com` and click on **My Account**. You might need to login again. Scroll down to **Your App subscription key**. Copy the key, shown highlighted (on the right-hand side) in the following screenshot:

12. Now switch back to the browser tab containing the install progress report, we were on a moment ago. Scroll down to the **Weever App Subscription Key** section. Paste your key in the section, which is highlighted in the following screenshot.

13. Click on the **Submit Key** button as shown in the preceding screenshot.

How it works...

We are now ready to start building our app. We have installed the extension in the normal Joomla! manner, registered our site with `weeverapp.com` and copied and pasted our key to activate the component. Now we can get on with actually making an app from the Weever control panel as can be seen in the following screenshot:

See also

▶ The *Configuring a Weever App* recipe

▶ The *Wrapping our site in an Android WebView* recipe, in *Chapter 9, Blueprint – Making an Android App out of Your Site Content*

Configuring a Weever App

In this recipe we will actually make an app out of your website content and content you might have on social media sites.

Getting ready

This recipe assumes you have setup Weever Apps. This was covered in the recipe, *Installing Weever Apps*. It also assumes you have some content published and ready to use in your Joomla! catalogue. In particular we make use of an article category and a **Contact Us** page.

How to do it...

The benefits of Weever as mentioned before is how easy it is to configure and change. So here is how to do it.

1. From the Joomla! control panel navigate to **Components | Weever Mobile App**.

2. Here, the first thing we can do is add content from our articles. We can add just an article, just a category, or a combination. We will add a category of content by clicking on the **Category** button. Now, we can see the following screenshot:

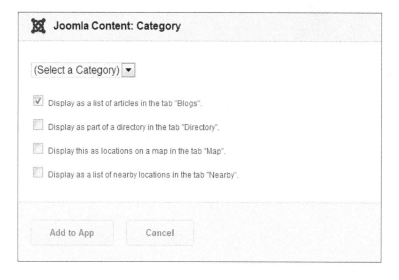

3. Click on the **(Select a Category)** dropdown and choose your category of articles that you want to be in your app. Click on **Add to App**.

4. Next we have another pop up box asking us to **Give this content a title** as shown in the following screenshot. You might want to give it the same title as the category but that is probably going to be too long. Try and make it one word if possible. You can experiment and come back and change it later if it is too long / could have been a bit longer. As the category we added was about search engine optimization I entered SEO.

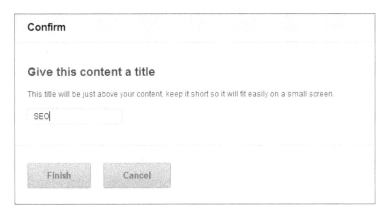

5. Click on **Finish**.

6. Now let's add a way for our app users to contact us . Click on the **Article** button.

Note there is an actual **Contact** button. But that adds an actual Joomla! contact into your app. This might or might not be what you want. What we are doing here is simply adding a page of content that just happens to be the **Contact Us** page. Obviously if you don't have a **Contact Us** page then you might want to add one. Or you can skip this step; your app will still wok just fine.

7. Click on the **Select** button. As you can see we choose the **Contact Us** article. But as with many steps in this recipe you can vary your choices. This can be seen in the following screenshot:

Title ≞	Access	Category	Language	Date	ID
3 reasons to use long tail keyword	Public	Category 1	All	2013-04-24	28
Contact Us	Public	Category 2	All	2013-04-05	25
Cool header	Public	Category 3	All	2013-04-10	27
New Page	Public	Subcategory 2a	All	2013-04-05	24
Slideshow	Public	Uncategorised	All	2013-04-10	26

8. Click on **Contact Us** and then click on **Add to app**. Like when we added a category earlier we need to come up with a nice short title to enter in the next pop up box. Type just `Contact` in the textfield with the flashing cursor. Now click on **Finish**.

9. Now we will add some social media links. Click on the **Add social media** tab. And then you can see something like the following screenshot:

10. Let's start with Facebook so click on the **Facebook** icon.

11. You are faced with a brief form to fill out as seen in the following screenshot. This won't take more than a minute. Enter the URL of your Facebook page. This is not the same thing as your Facebook profile. Now make sure all the options boxes are checked (as shown in the following screenshot) to allow your app users to view your photos and events.

12. Click on **Add to app**.

13. Now let's add some video content from Vimeo. Click on the **Add Audio, Video & Photos** tab then click on the **Vimeo** icon. Simply enter your Vimeo URL then click on **Add to app**. The suggested default title for this content **Video** as suggested by the next pop up box seems good. So click on **Finish**.

14. Repeat any of the preceding steps to add more content, social feeds, and so on to your app.

15. Click on the **Done** tab.

16. Now we can change what our app looks like. Click on the **Logo, Images and Theme** tab from the top row of main Weever tabs as shown in the following screenshot:

App Features + Navigation   Logo, Images and Theme   Mobile Publishing + Pro Features   Subscription Status + Staging Mode   Support

17. Here we have the opportunity to upload our graphics to make our app our own. Click on the **Your Logo Here** picture and upload your very own logo. Make sure the image is about the same ratio of length to width as the example and make sure it is as small a file size as possible. You can refer the following screenshot for this purpose:

18. Now do the same for the **Install Icon and Name**.

19. Choose an image suitable to act as an icon for your app on your customers phone screen. Enter a title to appear below that icon. **Cool App** would be a good title as shown in the following screenshot:

20. Now choose an image to replace the **Phone Loading Screen** image in the same way but by clicking on the **Phone Loading Screen** image.

21. Click on **Save Changes** near the top of the screen.

22. To use your app scan the QR code labeled **Test QR code** from the bottom of any of the Weever component tabs we just looked at. Scan it using any QR code scanner on any Android with Version 2.2 or higher or any iPhone as shown in the following screenshot:

 QR Droid is a popular and free QR code scanner available on Google Play.

How it works...

We added content from our site to our Weever App, defined a few graphics to be used and then we installed it. Now when someone visits your site or scans your QR code the Weever App content will be shown instead of the regular site.

See also

▸ The *Wrapping our site in an Android WebView* recipe, in *Chapter 9, Blueprint – Making an Android App out of Your Site Content*

Installing the VM Affiliate component

An affiliate is somebody who promotes or sells your products in return for a payment. The web affiliation is a very powerful tool because of the simplicity of linking from one domain to another. An affiliate can shout about the virtues of a product on another website and then link to that product giving his readers a direct link to make a purchase.

That's where the simplicity ends. If we want to reward the affiliate to make sure he keeps sending us great customers then we need to know which customers were sent by him and if they placed an order or not. In addition, how much did they spend? Do they become repeat customers? What merchandising material will our affiliates use? How do they know when our prices change? How does the affiliate know when he has made a sale? How does the affiliate know how much we owe him?

And many more questions besides. Affiliate campaign software abounds but almost all require fairly complex setup and management processes. Integration into Joomla! and VirtueMart can be troublesome at best and downright difficult at worst. Then because most affiliate software solutions are not meant specifically for Joomla! or VirtueMart there will always be some aspects that remain unsatisfactory. This causes extra work for us and uncertainty for affiliates. And affiliates hate uncertainty.

Enter VM Affiliate. VM Affiliate is a Joomla! component specifically written to integrate with VirtueMart. You install it (in about 60 seconds) and it just works. You will see as we progress through this and the next recipe as well that all the questions posed a couple of paragraphs back will be answered.

VM Affiliate is not free but it is not a significant investment for anyone serious about an affiliate campaign. You can investigate the full features at `www.globacide.com`.

Getting ready

Head over to `www.globacide.com` and login to your account, download VM Affiliate by clicking on the **Download** link as shown in the following screenshot:

Download the Version of VM Affiliate that is appropriate for your Version of Joomla! and VirtueMart. Here I have chosen Version 4.5 for Joomla! 2.5 and VirtueMart 2 as shown in the following screenshot:

| VM Affiliate 4.5: J!1.7/2.5 & VM 2.0 | 1126 KB | Mar 25, 2013 | 700 | ⬇ |

Put the file somewhere handy like your desktop and we will get started.

How to do it...

The real fun with VM Affiliate is setting up and running a campaign. Fortunately this bit before we get to the fun is super simple. So here we go.

1. From your Joomla! admin panel navigate to **Extensions | Extension Manager**.

2. In the **Upload Package File** area click on **Browse** and select your VM Affiliate download from your desktop. The file will be called something like, `VMA 4.5 for J!1.7-2.5 & VM2.0.zip`.

3. Now click on **Upload and Install**.

How it works...

In a couple of clicks we have installed the VM Affiliate component. And then you can see something like the following screenshot:

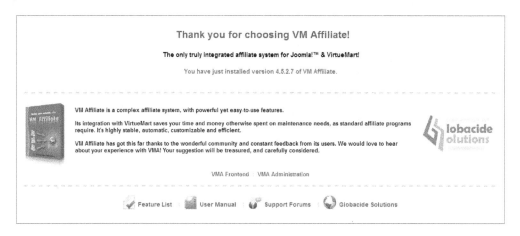

Now we have the ability to configure settings, start campaigns including adding products, banners, and so on, and accept new affiliates to sell our products for us in return for a commission.

- The *Setting up a campaign and testing it with VM Affiliate* recipe
- The *Harness the power of affiliates with Mijo* recipe, in *Chapter 8, VirtueMart Alternatives*

Setting up a campaign and testing it with VM Affiliate

Here's how it will all work when we are done:

- Affiliate marketers looking for new and exciting products to sell find your website.
- They see you have a generous commission structure and some good quality banners and promotional material.
- They join your program, login to their affiliate control panel (powered by VM Affiliate) and use the tools and material to promote your products on their website.
- Visitors come to your affiliates website and read glowing and informative information about your products. They click on a link and arrive on your website. If the visitor makes a purchase within a reasonable time period (definable by you) the affiliate is credited with the sale.
- Affiliate very happy to make money and redoubles his efforts to sell more of your products.

Getting ready

To enable all this functionality is surprisingly simple. Think about a few things to prepare for this recipe.

- Consider the way(s) you would like your affiliates to promote you. Including banners, text links and coupon codes.
- Consider how much, either as a percentage or a cash figure you would like to pay your affiliates per sale.
- Consider carefully how long after an affiliate sends a visitor to your site you would like them to still be rewarded for a sale. The default is set at one year. In most cases this is probably too long. A good rule of thumb is to base the time (cookie length) on the repeat nature of your products. If you sell consumable ink cartridges to businesses that change them every 2 months, you might not want to give your affiliate 6 commissions for one link through. You might only want to reward them for the first sale. If this is the case 1 month would be a good cookie length. On the other hand if you sell rarely purchased high priced items then a cookie length of 1 month will discourage many affiliates. Perhaps here you should consider a minimum of 3 months. Think about what will work best for your products.

> ▶ What type of materials do you want to provide to help your affiliates sell your products. Banners with your company and product range, banners with specific products, short paragraphs of promotional text, coupon codes, and so on. Prepare your materials.

Gather your information together and proceed when ready.

How to do it...

So let's click on a few buttons and we will be ready for new affiliates in no time. After that we will play the role of a new affiliate so we can check that everything is working.

Setting up our affiliate campaign:

1. Go to your VirtueMart control panel and look down at the left hand menu. Notice you have a new **Affiliates** option. Click on **Affiliates**. Here are the options we see (spread out horizontally in the following screenshot to avoid taking up a whole page).

2. First let's give our future affiliates some merchandising material to make their job as easy as possible. Click on **Banners** and then the **New** button in the top right.

3. Click on **Upload Banner** and choose your first promotional banner. You can refer the following screenshot for this purpose

4. Type a name for this banner in the Name field. I typed `Site wide banner`.

5. Now we can choose exactly what we want that banner to link to. If your banner was a general company banner it could point to the home page. Or category specific to the category page, and so on. Click on the **Link** dropdown list.

6. Notice we can not only choose specific products and product categories but also articles and article categories. This enables us to create a very fine tuned and precise campaign but potentially very flexible for our affiliates at the same time. Click on **Site** from the dropdown list to make this banner link to your site home page as shown in the preceding screenshot.

7. Click on **Save**.

8. Repeat steps 2 to 7 to add all the different banners linking to all the different places to suit your campaign.

9. Now from our recently acquired **Affiliates** menu click on **Text Ads**.

10. Click on the **New** button in the top right.

11. In the **Name** field type a name that accurately describes the purpose of this textual content we will create in a moment. I entered `Small shovel promotional snippet`.

12. In the **Text** field type some sales copy to entice visitors to your affiliates sites to click on and visit you. Note that despite the name of this type of asset (Text ads) you could also enter images, potentially creating an entire article. For the benefit of simplicity here and to make the **Size** option work better just stick to text for now.

13. As we did with the banners choose the location for this ad to link to by clicking on the **Link** dropdown and choosing the link target. In my case this is the **Smaller Shovel** link.

14. The next option, **Size** takes a bit of explaining. For this text ad we will keep it simple and leave it on **(Fluid)** but notice you could click on the dropdown and choose from a wide range of container sizes. By choosing appropriate container sizes you can influence where and how your text ad is displayed. Leaving it as **(Fluid)**, as we have, means the code that the future affiliate will copy and paste to his site will adapt to almost any space they choose to give it. If you decided to enter an image in step 12 then you should test your ad in different settings before choosing the **(Fluid)** option to make sure it looks good. Otherwise choose one of the fixed sizes. Refer the following screenshot to better understand the **Size** option:

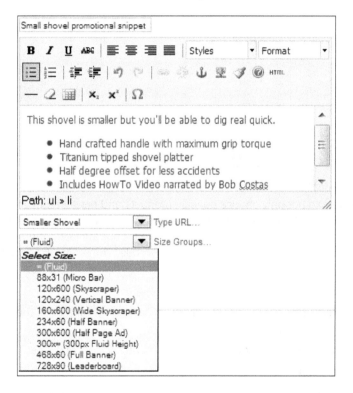

15. Click on **Save**.

16. Repeat steps 10 to 15 to add all your text ads.

17. Now let's set up how much our affiliates can earn. Click on **Commission Rates**.

18. Choose the type and value of the commission you will pay. Here we enter `10.00` in the **Percentage** field. We have chosen to pay a 10 percent commission on the value of the entire sale. The more the customer spends, the more the affiliate makes. We can see this in the following screenshot:

19. Click on **Save**.

20. We are nearly ready to launch and test our affiliate campaign. A few more clicks. Click on **Configuration** from the **Affiliates** menu.

21. Make sure that **Allow affiliate registrations** and **Automatically approve affiliates** both have a tick in their box as shown in the following screenshot:

22. Set the **Minimum Payout balance** to a figure that will not discourage smaller affiliates unless you want to discourage smaller affiliates. I suggest entering around `10.0` here unless you have a specific reason not too.

23. Choose a day of the month to automatically pay all your affiliates via PayPal. Here we have left it on the default of the 1st as shown in the following screenshot:

24. Click on **Save**.

Testing our affiliate campaign:

1. Visit your website homepage and you will notice that VM Affiliate has automatically added an **Affiliates** link to your main menu. Click on **Affiliates** as shown in the following screenshot:

2. Notice that VM Affiliate has done all the work for you. It has created a whole page that advertises to would-be affiliates, your rate, minimum payment, and payment day. It provides a place for existing affiliates to login and a link for people to sign up to become an affiliate. Click on the **Become an Affiliate!** link as shown in the following screenshot:

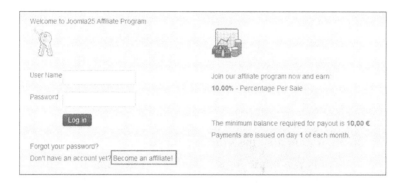

3. Fill out the self explanatory registration form. Perhaps use your own personal details for testing and click on **Register Now** at the bottom of the form. Then you will see a success message, something like the following screenshot:

Congratulations! You have successfully signed up for our affiliate program!

4. You will receive an e-mail to your Joomla! administrators e-mail address telling you that you have your first affiliate and you will receive an e-mail to the address that you used when registering as an affiliate. In the latter of the two e-mails is a link to the affiliate login page. Let's click on that now and login. And you will see something like the following screenshot.

5. You can see we have a lot of options. At the top of the page you might have noticed the message **You haven't selected any payment method. Please take some time to do so.** Click on the message.

6. Here you can see all the ways an affiliate can be paid. The simplest is to just enter the e-mail address associated with your PayPal account and then every time the affiliate has a balance in excess of the minimum on the pay date we configured it will just work. It is this easy because VM Affiliate is integrated into VirtueMart and can use some of the VirtueMart configurations. It is true that there are some even better featured affiliate software and I have mentioned them in the Resources appendix. But VM Affiliate is the easiest by a very long way, it is keenly priced and the features are quite good also. Configure your payment by entering your PayPal details in the **PayPal E-mail** box and check the **PayPal** radio button as well as shown in the following screenshot. And then click on **Save**.

7. From the row of links at the top of this page click on the **Affiliate panel** link to return to the main set of options.

8. Let's explore further to understand the experience our future affiliates will have and how they might implement a campaign. Click on **Banners & Ads**.

9. Here we can see all the banners and text links that we made. And if we look closely under the **HTML code** heading, as shown in the preceding screenshot, we can see the actual code that needs to be copied and pasted on the affiliates website. I have copied and pasted it as follows, so we can take a look at it. Notice that near the end of the second line of code is the text ...aff_id=1... This is how VM Affiliate will keep track of sales and who sent them to us. If you have another website paste the code into it as well and try clicking on the link.

```
<a href="http:// hadronwebdesign.co.uk/index.php?banner_
id=1&amp;aff_id=1">

<img src="http:// hadronwebdesign.co.uk/components/com_affiliate/
banners/ea5ee1c7fe89c48ce17ba8e7385235fa.png" alt="Ad" /></a>
```

10. Click on the **Affiliate Panel** link and notice that an affiliate can track their **Traffic**, **Sales**, **Payments**, and **General statistics**. Click on each in turn and see what they offer your affiliates. All the data is in real time. As a click is made or a sale paid, VM Affiliate updates the relevant parts of the affiliate control panel. This is vital because it creates transparency and trust. Without which no affiliate will work for you for long.

How it works...

By configuring all the options that we have and making available all the promotional material for our future affiliates we have made it very easy for someone to join your scheme and start promoting your products on their sites.

By testing the experience a new affiliate will have, we are ready to support them should they need to contact us and we understand the experience they have preparing to promote our products.

8

VirtueMart Alternatives

In this chapter we will cover:

- ▸ Installing HikaShop as an alternative to VirtueMart
- ▸ HikaShop quick evaluation tour
- ▸ Installing RedShop as an alternative to VirtueMart
- ▸ RedShop quick evaluation tour
- ▸ Installing J2Store for in-article products
- ▸ Configuring J2Store
- ▸ Adding a product to a Joomla! article with J2Store
- ▸ Installing MyMuse for digital download products
- ▸ Configuring MyMuse
- ▸ Adding products to MyMuse

Introduction

In this chapter we look at four Joomla! e-commerce components. The first two HikaShop and RedShop stand as fully fledged e-commerce solutions and potential alternatives to VirtueMart.

The next two perform very specific aspects really well. J2Store allows you to have products and cart neatly integrated into a Joomla! article, the second MyMuse facilitates the selling of digital files and is especially well suited to music downloads. They are not replacements for full VirtueMart functionality and they do not integrate with VirtueMart but do seem to work nicely alongside but separate to VirtueMart.

Installing HikaShop as an alternative to VirtueMart

Be sure to check the demo and up-to-date features list online at `www.hikashop.com`. You can try the free starter version of HikaShop, to see if you like the feel of it, but the next recipe will use features, modules, and extensions of the paid versions.

Getting ready

Buy/download the version of HikaShop that is right for you. If you are going with the free starter version for now you can get that at `http://www.hikashop.com/en/download.html`. Just click on the big green **Download** button shown in the following screenshot:

Put the contents of the download you just got from hikashop.com on your desktop and find the file `hikashop.zip`.

How to do it...

It is nice and simple to get started with HikaShop, so let's do it:

1. From your Joomla! control panel select **Extensions | Extension Manager**.
2. In the **Upload Package File** area click on the **Browse** button and select the downloaded `hikashop.zip` file. Now click on **Upload File and Install**.
3. We now have a big long list of all the successful installations of the various components of HikaShop and if we scroll to the bottom we see the success/welcome message from the Hikari Software team as shown in the following screenshot:

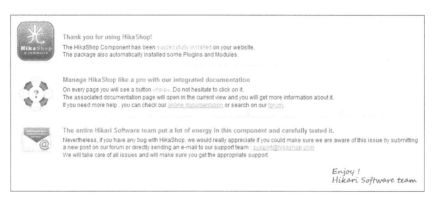

4. Now let's add a link to our new HikaShop from our site's main menu. Select **Menus | Main Menu | Add New Menu Item**.

5. Next to the **Menu Item Type** field at the top of the page click on **Select**. Scroll down until you see the list of HikaShop menu types as shown in the following screenshot:

HikaShop

User addresses
Affiliate program
Cart Display
Cart listing
Categories listing
Checkout
Entry registration
Customer orders
Comparison page
Contact page
Products listing
Product page
User control panel
Registration form

6. Select **Categories listing**.

7. In the **Menu Title** field, type The Shop.

8. Click on **Save**.

9. Now we have saved our progress, a new option presents itself. On the right of the page under **HikaShop Options** click on the **HikaShop options** link. Now we see the following screenshot near the top of the page:

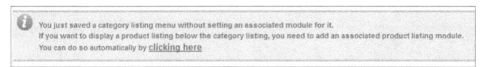

You just saved a category listing menu without setting an associated module for it.
If you want to display a product listing below the category listing, you need to add an associated product listing module.
You can do so automatically by clicking here

10. To have HikaShop finish the configuration of this menu item click on the **clicking here** link. You can see it in the preceding screenshot.

11. Click on **Save & Close**.

How it works...

The basics of HikaShop are now ready to go and we have a main menu link to our store, albeit an empty store.

See also

▸ The *HikaShop quick evaluation tour* recipe

HikaShop quick evaluation tour

HikaShop could be the topic of a whole book and it could never be done justice in a couple of recipes. This recipe will be a fast and furious look at some of the features that HikaShop has to offer, to help you evaluate its worth to you or your clients.

Getting ready

Go to our HikaShop control panel by selecting **Components** | **HikaShop**. We will start from here. The page will look like the following screenshot:

How to do it...

Let's look at some of the in-depth configurations and cool options of HikaShop:

1. One of the most striking things in HikaShop that you just don't get in your average shopping cart software is built-in affiliate management. Hover over the **Affiliates** tab (as seen in the following screenshot) to see our options here. This is a significant addition for any business that intends to promote itself using affiliate campaigns. And as alluded to in the previous recipe, this is a feature not available in the free version.

Following are the features provided by the **Affiliates** tab:

- ❏ You can quickly monitor and delete affiliates
- ❏ Add banners and other sales aids for your affiliates to use
- ❏ Monitor exactly which sales were sent by which affiliates

2. There are vastly more configurable reporting options in HikaShop compared to VirtueMart as shown in the following screenshot:

3. And you can add and customize your own reports as well, as shown in the following screenshot:

4. There is even a global heat map report as shown in the following screenshot:

5. These options can be found under **Configuration | Features**. Wish lists are a really nice feature and proven to improve customer retention. HikaShop comes with a highly configurable wish list module as shown in the following screenshot:

6. Import from VirtueMart directly from the VirtueMart database. This is really handy if you are migrating from VirtueMart. The page will look like the following screenshot:

How it works...

We looked at what are probably the top distinguishing things about HikaShop. It is fairly plain to see it offers some significant advantages over VirtueMart with the exception of the obvious one (the price) and one not so obvious.

The not so obvious one being that HikaShop is probably a fair bit more complex than VirtueMart to get going. But it is also reasonable to say that the depth of configuration options, feature list, and ease of use once mastered is better with HikaShop than with VirtueMart.

Having said what I did about price, if you look at the price for features like Affiliate software, Wish lists, Multi-vendor features, and so on when using VirtueMart, then HikaShop competes well with VirtueMart on price as well.

See also

▶ The *Installing RedShop as an alternative to VirtueMart* recipe
▶ The *RedShop Quick evaluation tour* recipe

Installing RedShop as an alternative to VirtueMart

RedShop is free but most if its components and modules are not. So you can download and try out the basic functionality before you decide if you want to make an investment. This recipe will help you install the basic components, the next will take you on a whirlwind tour of the free and paid aspects to help you decide if RedShop is for you.

Getting ready

Make a free account at `http://www.redcomponent.com/redcomponent/redshop`. Log in to your account and download the free RedShop. Put it on your desktop.

How to do it...

This recipe just uses the free download but the next recipe uses many of the paid for/pro license downloads:

1. In your Joomla! control panel select **Extensions | Extension Manager**.
2. Click on the **Browse** button and select the file `redSHOP-v1.2_25j.zip` that you just downloaded.

3. Click on **Upload and Install**.

4. Wait while RedShop installs. It takes around 5 minutes.

5. Click on the **install Demo Content** button, it will make exploring and evaluating RedShop much easier. The page will look like the following screenshot:

How it works...

Now you have the basic RedShop installed, you can explore its functionality. A quick glance at the extent of the control panel tells us there is much to explore.

See also

  ▸ The *RedShop quick evaluation tour* recipe

RedShop quick evaluation tour

Just what the title says. We will look at some of the basic RedShop features on the shop front and then some of the paid features.

Getting ready

Install RedShop by following the previous recipe.

How to do it...

Follow along for a while in the free version but this recipe also looks at the paid features as well:

1. Let's take a look at the shop front. To do that we will create a main menu link to the store. In your Joomla! control panel select **Menus | Main Menu | Add New Menu Item**.

2. Click on **Select** by the **Menu Item Type** label and scroll down to the **RedShop** options. As we can see in the following screenshot they are quite extensive.

3. Select **Standard Category Detail Layout**.

4. Enter RedShop in the **Menu Title** field.

5. On the right-hand side of the screen in the **Select Category*** dropdown choose the category **-redCOMPONENT** as shown in the following screenshot:

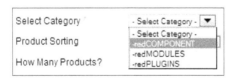

6. Click on **Save & Close**.

7. In the frontend click on the new menu item pointing to RedShop.

8. There are multiple product option types on one product. Notice the subscription dropdown and the add-on checkboxes combined, as shown in the following screenshot. The price reacts dynamically to them all.

RedEvent is, as the name suggests is an event management system. It can take bookings and collate data into various formats. Take a look at the events and event filters shown in the following screenshot:

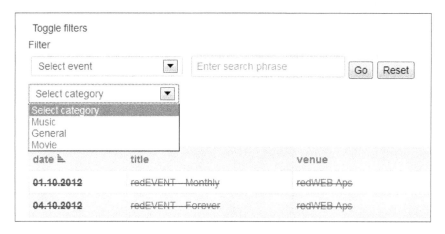

The RedEvent component is free but if you want integration of payments, the following nifty Calendar module, or one of more than a dozen cool event extensions then you will need to buy them.

Unfortunately this is where the free stuff ends. Just about every payment method you can imagine can be integrated into RedShop including all the major gateways from Amazon to SagePay as well as multiple bank transfer options, so you can have more than one bank transfer option set up at the same time.

Other noteworthy features include integration with the excellent and free PHPList. Run an e-mail campaign with no monthly fees and with closer integration than any of the big name providers can offer you. Even with a payment of 60 Euros per month (based on 10,000 e-mails), this add-on is just $24 as a one off payment!

Redshop contains very neat featured product, manufacturer, and category slide shows ($24 each).

It also offers neat social recommendations such as wish lists and customers who bought modules ($24 each).

How it works...

In our quick tour we looked at selective RedShop extensions, both free and paid. We saw some product options and it probably needs to be mentioned they were not buggy and awkward, like we saw with some of the custom fields we configured with VirtueMart in *Chapter 2, Merchandising VirtueMart*.

On the upside, with VirtueMart, you can google most VirtueMart problems, less so with RedShop. Although they do have a forum with around 200,000 members and if you buy the pro license, support is included!

I think it is fairly plain to see that RedShop is significantly better featured as well as more pleasing to use for an admin as compared to VirtueMart.

Clearly there is no best solution, but there will likely be a solution that best matches yours or your client's situation. Probably a fair summary would be that, if your project has the budget, RedShop will give you much over and above VirtueMart, but a careful assessment of VirtueMart shows that if VirtueMart will do, then you can save a few hundred dollars.

Also, if you do go with RedShop you are almost certainly better off just going for the Pro option straight away and getting everything included. The vast array of add-ons, extensions, and modules will soon take you past the Pro fee and you will also get technical support.

See also

▶   The *Installing HikaShop as an alternative to VirtueMart* recipe

Installing J2Store for in-article products

J2Store is not a regular e-commerce component. It has some very specific features that make it ideal in very specific circumstances. It can display and sell inside an actual Joomla! article.

J2Store is free but all the payment modules need to be paid for. If you wanted to connect J2Store to PayPal, for example, you would need to pay $25 (at the time of writing). What makes this situation easy to handle is that we can install and set up J2Store and fully test it out before we make this modest financial commitment.

Getting ready

Make sure you have some published categories ready for the article we will use with J2Store soon. If not, see the *Creating categories in Joomla!* and *Creating articles in Joomla!* recipes in *Chapter 6, Killer SEO*.

How to do it...

This is nice and easy. J2Store is not like other carts and we will soon have it installed and ready to play with:

1. Visit `http://j2store.org/downloads.html`. The page will look like the following screenshot:

2. Download the latest stable version of J2Store by clicking on the link indicated in the preceding screenshot. It will probably be a different version number by the time you read this. Put the file somewhere easy to find, like on your desktop.

3. In your Joomla! control panel select **Extensions | Extension Manager**, then in the area labeled **Upload Package File**, click on the **Browse** button and select the file you just downloaded. In this example it is called `com_j2store-2.0.2-core.zip`. Click on **Upload and Install**. Wait for the install process to complete.

How it works...

We have just installed J2Store in the usual Joomla! way. Now the fun can begin.

See also

▶   The *Configuring J2Store* recipe

Configuring J2Store

Here we will do the basic configuration of J2Store making it ready for the next recipe, when we will actually add a product in a Joomla! article.

Getting ready

Just read on to get the basic J2Store configuration ready.

How to do it...

J2Store is a well thought out component. It doesn't try to clobber us with unnecessary features. This makes what we are about to do really simple. So let's do it:

1. In the main Joomla! menu select **Components | J2Store**.
2. Click on the **Options** button.

Options

3. Click on the **Shop Settings** tab. Enter your e-mail address, name, and shop name in the appropriately labeled fields.
4. Click on the **Currency and Date** tab. The page will look like the following screenshot:

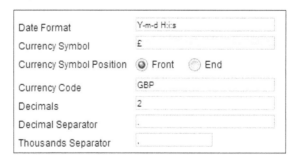

Date Format	Y-m-d H:i:s
Currency Symbol	£
Currency Symbol Position	⦿ Front ○ End
Currency Code	GBP
Decimals	2
Decimal Separator	.
Thousands Separator	,

5. If different from the default (US Dollars) enter the currency symbol and currency code for your currency in the **Currency Symbol** and **Currency Code** field boxes.
6. Click on **Save** then **Cancel**.

How it works...

Now we have the bare minimum configuration in place so that we can add our first product.

See also

▸ The *Adding a product to a Joomla! article with J2Store* recipe

Adding a product to a Joomla! article with J2Store

At last we will actually see J2Store in action in this recipe.

Getting ready

Have some product details like description and images ready and we will quickly get it done.

How to do it...

J2Store is simplicity itself. In around 5 minutes you can have your product available for sale. Compare that to VirtueMart which took around five chapters:

1. From the main Joomla! menu select **Content | Article Manager | Add New Article**.

2. Write/paste in your article and add it to the appropriate categories. Just as we did in *Creating articles in Joomla!* in *Chapter 6, Killer SEO*. This time, however, your article should be more than just an article. It should also be the description and any other information you wish to convey about the product, as shown in the following screenshot:

3. Now click on the **J2Store Cart** drop-down menu on the right-hand side of the page as shown in the following screenshot:

4. All we have to do is enter a price for our product and select the **Yes** radio button for **Enable cart** as indicated in the following screenshot:

5. Click on **Save** and we are done.

How it works...

J2Store does only one thing, products in articles, but it does it superbly. Notice that in this and the previous recipe there were more fine tuning options that we could have used such as tax, checkout field options, and even product attributes.

The following screenshot is what our article looks like to our visitors:

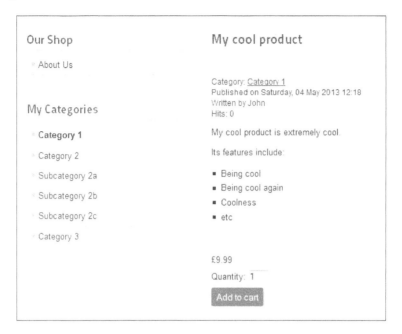

And the shopping cart looks like the following screenshot:

Installing MyMuse for digital download products

As with J2Store, MyMuse is not a replacement for VirtueMart. It is very good at one thing, selling digital downloads. In this recipe we will simply install MyMuse and in later recipes we will make it do something interesting.

MyMuse is not free. It costs $50 for a license and 6 months support and updates. We will hopefully see enough of MyMuse in this recipe to decide if it is the right solution for your digital downloads store.

Getting ready

Head over to www.mymuse.ca to purchase a license or read this and the next 2 recipes to evaluate if MyMuse is for you.

How to do it...

Ready to get your music store off the ground? Then follow the given steps:

1. Download the file com_mymuse_J25-2.5.3-994.zip from the www.mymuse.ca website after subscribing. Put it somewhere convenient, like on your desktop.

2. From the main Joomla! menu select **Extensions | Extension Manager**.

3. In the **Upload Package File** area click on **Browse** and select the file com_mymuse_ J25-2.5.3-994.zip. Now click on **Upload and Install**.

4. Wait until you see the following message:

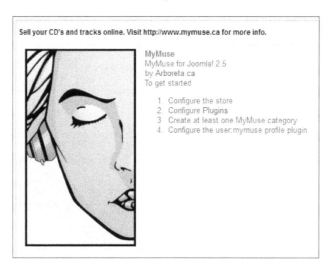

How it works...

We installed MyMuse in the usual Joomla! way. Now we can go and configure it.

See also

- ▸ The *Configuring MyMuse* recipe
- ▸ The *Adding products to MyMuse* recipe

Configuring MyMuse

Here we will enter the basic shop configuration options so that in the next recipe we are ready to add our first digital download.

Getting ready

Log in to your Joomla! control panel and read on.

How to do it...

We will quickly add the essential configurations:

1. Click on **Components | MyMuse** then click on the **Shop** tab.

2. Enter a name for your store in the **Title** field as shown in the following screenshot:

3. Enter a description for your store in the **Description** field as shown in the following screenshot:

4. Enter all your details in the **Contact** dropdown on the right, select your country from the **Country** dropdown, and choose your currency from the **Currency** dropdown, all within the **Contact** section.

5. Click on **Save & Close**.

6. Now we need to make our music store accessible to our site visitors by adding a menu item. Select **Menu | Main Menu | Add New Menu Item**.

7. Click on the **Select** button to add a new **Menu Item Type**. Scroll down until you see the MyMuse options as shown in the following screenshot:

8. Choose **List All MyMuse Categories**.

9. In the **Menu Title** field enter Music Shop.

10. Click on **Save & Close**.

How it works...

MyMuse has plenty of options but most of them are set to defaults which will work out of the box. The others we have just configured.

See also

▶ The *Adding products to MyMuse* recipe

Adding products to MyMuse

Having just opened our first digital music download store we had better add some products to it.

Getting ready

Have your mp3 files in a convenient place ready for uploading.

 You can also add short play samples. These need to be prepared as separate files.

How to do it...

We will quickly add some categories, a product and a track:

1. In the Joomla! control panel select **Components** | **MyMuse** and then click on the **Categories** tab.

2. Click on the **New** button.

3. Enter a title in the **Title** field as shown in the following screenshot:

4. Enter a description of this category in the **Description** field as shown in the following screenshot:

5. Click on **Save & Close**.

6. Repeat steps 2-5 to create all your categories.

7. Click on the **Products** tab.

8. Click on the **New** button.

9. In the **Title** field enter the title of the song.

10. In the **Main Category** dropdown select your category that the song belongs to.

11. Enter an SKU in the **SKU** field. This is mandatory in **MyMuse** unlike in VirtueMart.

12. In the **Product Physical** dropdown select **No** as shown in the following screenshot:

13. In the **Description** field describe the song as shown in the following screenshot:

14. Click on **Save**. We are not done yet. We just saved our progress to activate options on the other tabs.

15. Click on the **Tracks** tab. Click on **New Track**. The page will look like the following screenshot:

16. Enter the title of the track in the **Title*** field and the SKU in the **SKU*** field.

17. Click on **Browse** and select your audio file.

18. In the **File Time** field enter the running length of your track. For example, **3.24**.

19. Enter a price in the **Price** field.

20. On the right-hand side of the screen click on the **Browse** button and upload a preview of the track as shown in the following screenshot:

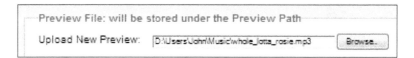

21. Click on **Save & Close**.

22. Repeat steps 8-21 for all your songs.

How it works...

First we created some categories, then some products, and then assigned a track to the products.

> You could have assigned multiple tracks to a product if your product was an album for instance.

The following screenshot displays the Whole Lotta Rosie track we configured in the preceding section:

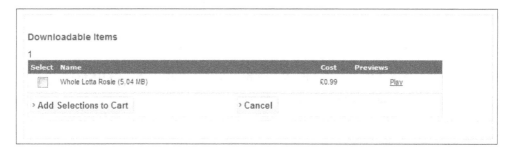

The following screenshot displays what the MyMuse shopping cart looks like with my dummy song in it:

Shopping Cart				
Title	Price	Quantity	Subtotal	Action
Hard : Whole Lotta Rosie : Whole Lotta Rosie	£0.99	1	£0.99	Delete
		Total:	£0.99 GBP	
			› Update Cart	
› Checkout		› Continue Shopping		

9
Blueprint – Making an Android App out of Your Site Content

In this chapter we will cover:

- ▶ Installing the Java Development Kit
- ▶ Installing Eclipse
- ▶ Installing the Android SDK
- ▶ Installing the Android Development Tools plugin
- ▶ Configuring an Android emulator
- ▶ Wrapping our site in an Android WebView
- ▶ Testing our app on the emulator
- ▶ Exporting our app to use it on a real Android device
- ▶ Branding our WebView
- ▶ Publishing our app on Google Play

Introduction

Apps are huge and are getting bigger. The proliferation of tablets and smart phones is likely a done deal and will never reverse. Most of the big name shopping brands have an app. But if you have ever shopped around for a service to make you an app you will probably have been scared off by the price.

But the good news is that getting a smart looking app for your business doesn't have to cost anything except a bit of time.

There are lots of advantages to having your own app as follows:

- It is another way to keep your products in your customers mind. An icon on their smart phone is a constant reminder and a click away from your latest special offer or article.

- Publishing on Google Play is yet another channel to be utilized. I know people who spend more time searching for apps than they do for websites. If your products are not in an app they might never find you.

- Credibility, that is, having a shiny "Get our app on Google Play" badge on your website gives the impression that you are a forward thinking company and because of the perceived high cost of entry into the world of branded apps, might make them think you are a bigger player than you really are.

Some broad statistics which I often tell my customers is that in 2012:

- Desktop searches declined for the first time ever

- One third of searches are on mobile devices

- Up to half of mobile searches are through an app

Although this is just a chapter, in all likelihoods, if you are totally new to this, you probably need to set aside a spare day to go from nothing all the way through to a published app. But you can easily do it a recipe at a time over a longer period if you prefer.

If you have any previous experience with the Java programming language you will probably be able to speed up things a bit as well as add extra enhancements along the way.

If you have programmed in any of the main languages of the web, perhaps JavaScript or PHP then Java will not trouble you and you should find it fairly simple to follow along.

If you have never programmed in any language before it doesn't matter, every step will be explained and even if you don't understand any of the code you can still make a cool app by copying and pasting when advised to do so.

Installing the Java Development Kit

The first stage is to set up the **Java Development Kit** (**JDK**). The JDK enables us to write programs that run in a Java Virtual Machine a bit like the one on every Android device and on virtually every PC or laptop.

Getting ready

This recipe is simply a matter of getting the right file, downloading it and going through the step by step installation process.

How to do it...

This is nice and easy taken a step at a time. First let's find the download.

1. Visit the oracle website to download the JDK at the URL `http://www.oracle.com/technetwork/java/javase/downloads/index.html`.

2. Scroll down the page and find the following section:

3. Click on the **DOWNLOAD** button underneath **JDK** as indicated in the preceding screenshot. If you scroll down a bit you can now see all the JDK download options as shown in the following screenshot:

Java SE Development Kit 7u21

You must accept the Oracle Binary Code License Agreement for Java SE to download this software.

○ Accept License Agreement   ◉ Decline License Agreement

Product / File Description	File Size	Download
Linux ARM v6/v7 Soft Float ABI	65.09 MB	jdk-7u21-linux-arm-sfp.tar.gz
Linux x86	80.35 MB	jdk-7u21-linux-i586.rpm
Linux x86	93.06 MB	jdk-7u21-linux-i586.tar.gz
Linux x64	81.43 MB	jdk-7u21-linux-x64.rpm
Linux x64	91.81 MB	jdk-7u21-linux-x64.tar.gz
Mac OS X x64	144.18 MB	jdk-7u21-macosx-x64.dmg
Solaris x86 (SVR4 package)	135.84 MB	jdk-7u21-solaris-i586.tar.Z
Solaris x86	92.08 MB	jdk-7u21-solaris-i586.tar.gz
Solaris x64 (SVR4 package)	22.67 MB	jdk-7u21-solaris-x64.tar.Z
Solaris x64	15.02 MB	jdk-7u21-solaris-x64.tar.gz
Solaris SPARC (SVR4 package)	136.09 MB	jdk-7u21-solaris-sparc.tar.Z
Solaris SPARC	95.44 MB	jdk-7u21-solaris-sparc.tar.gz
Solaris SPARC 64-bit (SVR4 package)	22.97 MB	jdk-7u21-solaris-sparcv9.tar.Z
Solaris SPARC 64-bit	17.58 MB	jdk-7u21-solaris-sparcv9.tar.gz
Windows x86	88.98 MB	jdk-7u21-windows-i586.exe
Windows x64	90.57 MB	jdk-7u21-windows-x64.exe

4. Click on the radio button at the top of the list of downloads next to **Accept License Agreement** then click on the link in the **Download** column for your operating system. I have highlighted the 64 bit version for Windows 7, `jdk-7u21-windows-x64.exe` as seen in the preceding screenshot The ...**u21**... aspect of this link might well have changed by the time you read this.

5. When prompted click on **Save the file**.

6. When the file is downloaded double click on `jdk-7u21-windows-x64.exe` to run it.

7. Click on **Next** as shown in the following screenshot:

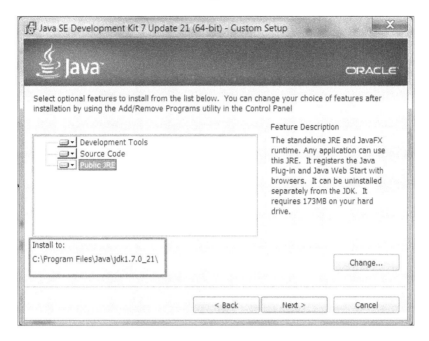

8. On this screen we can accept all the default settings but just note the file path, perhaps write it down, that is highlighted in the preceding screenshot. Here the path is C:\Program Files\Java\jdk_1.7.0_21\. This is were the JDK is being installed and we will need this information soon.

9. Click on **Next** and let Java do its thing.

10. You will be prompted to accept a location for installation of the **Java Runtime Environment** (**JRE**). This is the part of Java which actually runs the programs we create with the JDK. Select the default by clicking on **Next**.

11. When the installation completes click on the **Close** button.

12. Here are the final steps. We need to tell Windows what we did. We have the latest versions of the JDK and the JRE on our system. We need to let Windows know that for all Java related things; please use them. Click on the Windows Start button. The page will look like the following screenshot:

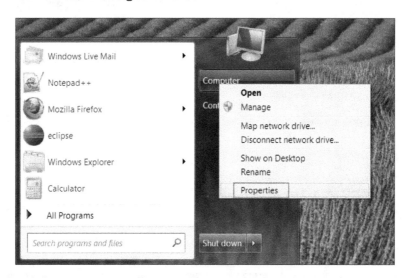

13. Right click on **Computer** and select **Properties**.

14. Click on **Advanced system settings** and then **Environment Variables**.

15. In the **System variables** window scroll down to the line that starts with **JAVA_HOME** as shown in the following screenshot:

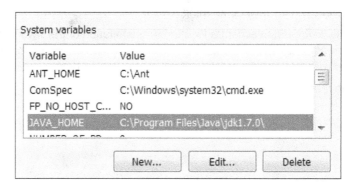

16. Click on the **JAVA_HOME** line and then click on **Edit...**. Enter the folder path that you copied in step 8 into the resulting edit box. The following screenshot depicts the same but enter your folder path, not necessarily the exact same one as in this example.

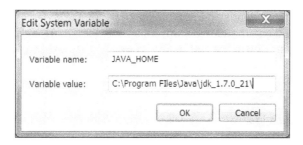

 If you do not have a **JAVA_HOME** line simply click on the **New** button instead of the **JAVA_HOME** line in step 16 and enter the **Variable name:** and **Variable value:** exactly as it is in the preceding image but substituting the **Variable value:** for your exact folder path you recorded in step 8. Click on **Save** to save your new variable and continue with the recipe.

17. In the **Environment Variables** window find the line that starts with **Path**.

18. Click on it and then on **Edit**. With your cursor keys, scroll to the very end of the edit box. Be sure not to change anything. When you reach the end of all the text add a semicolon ; and then %JAVA_HOME% as shown in the following screenshot:

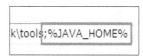

19. Click on **Save**.

20. Click on the **OK** button.

How it works...

We downloaded the latest versions of the Java Development Kit so that we can write Java programs. Contained as part of that download was also the JRE which runs Java programs. We then did the slightly fiddly task of telling Windows to check the folder where we installed this new Java stuff so the whole thing works.

Installing Eclipse

Eclipse is an **Integrated Development Environment** (**IDE**) and it is the IDE of choice for many Android developers simply because it integrates a lot of complexity and avoids us having to learn lots of complicated command-line stuff, which is a good thing. Eclipse is what makes all the things we are installing in the last recipe as well as the next two, work together.

Getting ready

Before we start, make a folder where we will do all our Android work. I suggest keeping it simple and quickly accessible. So make a folder called `Android` on the root of your main hard drive. In our case it is `C:\Android` as shown in the following screenshot:

How to do it...

This is much quicker and easier than the previous recipe.

1. Visit `http://www.eclipse.org/downloads/` and scroll down to find the Classic version of Eclipse as shown in the following screenshot:

2. Download the 64 Bit version for 64 Bit Windows 7 by clicking on the link **Windows 64 Bit**.

3. You will be shown a default download link for your country. Click on it to download the file `eclipse-SDK-4.2.2-win32-x86_64.zip`. Put the file on the desktop.

4. Extract the file `eclipse-SDK-4.2.2-win32-x86_64.zip` by right clicking on it and selecting **Extract Here**.

5. Move the resulting Eclipse folder and its entire contents into the `C:\Android` we created while getting ready for this recipe.

How it works...

That is it. There is no actual installation program for Eclipse. Go to `C:\Android\Eclipse` and double click on `eclipse.exe` to take a peek at the IDE we will be using soon. It will ask you to choose a default workspace. You can just accept the default. The page will look like the following screenshot:

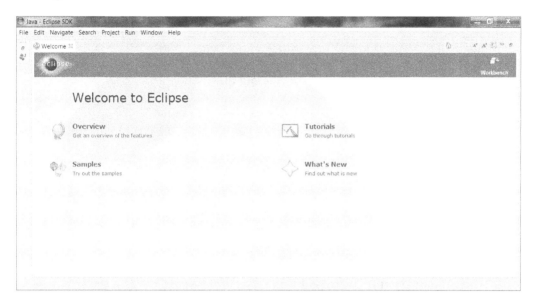

Installing the Android SDK

The Android **Software Development Kit** (**SDK**) is what lets us write Java programs for Android. The SDK enables us to do apparently complicated Android stuff really easily.

Getting ready

Visit the link `http:/developer.android.com/sdk/` and read on. The page will look like the following screenshot:

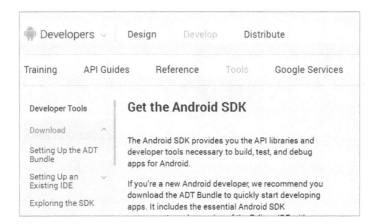

How to do it...

You shouldn't break a sweat doing this. So here it goes.

1. Scroll down to **Use an existing IDE** and click on **Download the SDK tools for Windows**.

2. Check the box next to **I have read and agree to the above terms and conditions**. Click on the **Download SDK tools for Windows** button.

3. When completed run the download by double clicking on `installer_r21.1-windows.exe`. Accept all the default options until you get to the screen, **Choose Install location**.

4. Type `C:\Android\android-sdk` as shown in the following screenshot:

5. Click on **Next** and then **Next** again.

6. When you get to the **Completing the Android SDK tools setup wizard** uncheck the **Start SDK Manager (to download system images, etc.)** checkbox as shown in the following screenshot:

7. Then click on **Finish**.

How it works...

The SDK is potentially everything a developer needs to get started but because we want to use the SDK via the nice friendly Eclipse IDE we have one more recipe to go before we can start doing Android things.

See also

  ▸   The *Installing the Android Development Tools plugin* recipe

Installing the Android Development Tools plugin

The plugin is what makes Eclipse hook up with the Android SDK. Just one more set of mind numbing install screens and we will be ready to do something more fun, I promise.

Getting ready

Close down all programs on your PC and be to ready to install the plugin. We will get Eclipse to connect to the download site and then install the ADT plugin into itself.

How to do it...

This step is nice and simple. Just follow along the following steps:

1. Start Eclipse by going to `C:\Android\Eclipse` and double click on `eclipse.exe`.

2. Click on **Help | Install New Software**.

3. The **Available Software** dialog will pop up. In the top right click on the **Add...** button as shown in the following screenshot:

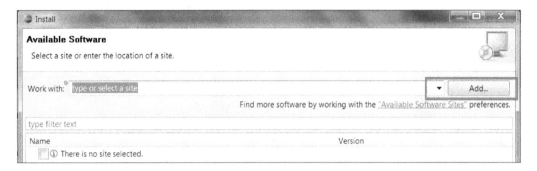

4. In the next pop up enter `ADT Plugin` in the **Name** field and enter the URL `https://dl-ssl.google.com/android/eclipse/` in the **Location** field. As shown in the following screenshot:

5. Now click on the **OK** button.
6. In the **Available Software** dialog, check the checkbox next to **Developer Tools**.
7. Click on **Next**.
8. Click on **Next** again.
9. Click on **Finish**.
10. If you get a security warning you can safely ignore it just click on **OK**.
11. Now shut Eclipse down by clicking on the Red **X** in the top right and then restart it again by visiting the usual location by double clicking on `eclipse.exe`.
12. Select **Window | Preferences | Android** from the top Eclipse menu as shown in the following screenshot:

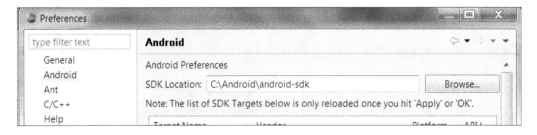

13. By the field labeled **SDK Location:** click on the **Browse** button and browse to where we put your SDK in the previous recipe, **C:\Android\android-sdk**.

14. Click on **OK** and relax.

How it works...

We have just integrated Eclipse with the Android SDK by installing the ADT plugin and letting Eclipse know where the SDK is.

Configuring an Android emulator

Throughout the rest of this chapter we will need to test our app as we develop new features. It is always advisable to test your app every time you do anything significant to it.

Creating an actual Android compatible file (`.apk`) and then installing it on a phone is quite a lengthy process. Also the emulator has some tools for debugging our app although we won't be going into those features in this book.

The other advantage of an emulator is you can create multiple different emulators for different versions of Android as well as for different devices. So it is nice and simple to test our users experience without owning dozens of phones and tablets.

Getting ready

Make sure Eclipse is fired up and ready to go.

How to do it...

At last we will be doing something with visible results. By the end of this recipe you will have a working Android emulator that you can actually do Android like things on. So let's do it.

1. In Eclipse select **Window | Android Virtual Device Manager**.

2. Now click on the **New** button and we will configure a virtual device (emulator).

3. In the **AVD Name:** field type `Android_4_Phone`. Don't miss out the underscores.

4. Click on the **Device:** dropdown and select **5.1" WVGA (480 x 800: mdpi)**.

5. In **Target** select **Android 4.2 – API Level 17**. The page will look like the following screenshot:

6. Click on **OK** and we have an emulator for a rather cool, if rather large phone.

How it works...

In a few clicks we configured an Android emulator. Want to try it out? Of course you do.

 Warning! The first time the emulator starts up it will take a long time. I mean a really long time. So start it up and come back in 10 minutes (or more) to have a play with it. When you are done, if you are proceeding with the next recipe straight away then leave it running.

1. Select **Window | Android Virtual Device Manager**. The page will look like the following screenshot:

⌄ Android_4_P...	Android 4.0	4.0	14	ARM (armeabi...

2. Choose our recently created emulator by clicking on it and click on **Start**.
3. Have a coffee.
4. Have a click around and explore. The page will look like the following screenshot:

Wrapping our site in an Android WebView

Now we get to the bit where we actually start making an app. The Android code that we will write is in the Java language. It will work on over 90 percent of Android devices.

What we will do in this recipe is, create a wrapper for our site content. So it will be like making a web browser app but a web browser app that only has our site in it. It will be fully compatible and testable and we will do so at the end of the recipe in the *How it works...* section.

As you will see, we will also change the browser look and feel to make it more app like than just browser like.

Getting ready

When we create our Android project in just a few moments we will be asked to define a few things to get started. This includes a name for the app. Think of a name that is quite short, so it is not truncated on the screen of an Android phone and one that is obvious what it does.

We also get the opportunity to define the graphics that will be used as the start icon on the Android phones where our app is installed. You might like to have at hand some neat graphics ready for this purpose.

How to do it...

In around 10 minutes we will have the first iteration of our Android app.

1. Start Eclipse by going to `C:\Android\Eclipse` and double clicking on `eclipse.exe`. In future recipes I will simply say, start Eclipse.

2. Select **File | New | Android Application Project**.

3. Type your short application name in the **Application Name** field. Notice that Eclipse has filled out the other boxes for you. The second field **Project Name** will be the same as your application name but with spaces stripped out. Leave **Project Name** at the default.

4. The third field is the **Package name**. We need to change it to the following format. `<your top level domain>.<your domain name>.<your application name in lower case without spaces>`. An example would be useful. If our website is **www.hadronwebdesign.com** and the application is going to be called **Hadron Design** and the top level domain is **com**. The domain name is **hadronwebdesign**. And the application name without spaces and in lower case is **hadrondesign**. Now we put all that together and stick a period "**.**" between each section we get. **com.hadronwebdesign.hadrondesign**. The idea behind this slightly convoluted process is that we have a unique identifier for our project on Google Play that will likely never be repeated. Have a look at the following screenshot to see how things should look at this stage:

5. The rest of the settings we can leave at the default. Eclipse sets sensible oldest and newest target Android versions to make our application compatible with. Your defaults will probably be slightly different to mine in the screenshot. Click on **Next**.

6. The next screen we can leave all the defaults. We are basically telling Eclipse to write some code for us to get us started quickly and to give us the chance to upload our custom launcher icons that we discussed in the *Getting Ready* section. Double check whether your settings are the same as the following screenshot:

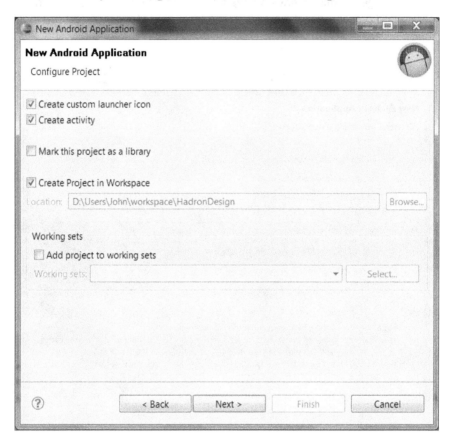

7. Click on **Next**.

8. The next screen looks complicated but it isn't. It is simply a little tool to help you design your launcher icons. Notice there are four default icons. Default in case you don't have your icons made yet and four because by supplying icons at different sizes Android can make them look and fit beautifully on the smallest phones and the biggest tablets.

9. You can choose to upload your custom images (recommended for the unique branded look, just click on **Browse** and select your image), keep the default (you would be surprised how many amateur app developers actually publish with the default icon set), choose to simply pick a stock Android clipart image(by clicking on **Clipart**), or simply use some Android styled text as your icon(by clicking on **Text**).

10. Decide what works best for you, play around a bit with the options and then read on. The configuration I chose is described in the next step and shown in the following screenshot:

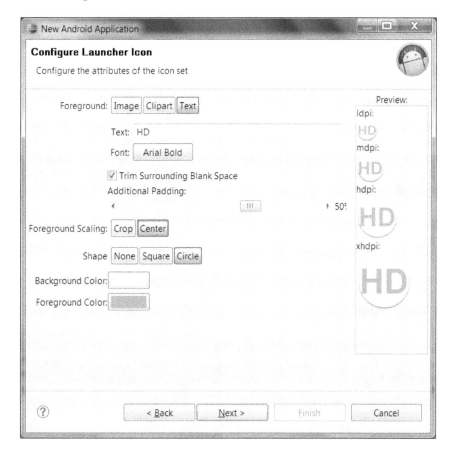

11. The effect above was achieved by selecting the **Text** button and entering HD in the **Text** field. Then choosing **Center** for **Foreground Scaling**, **Circle** for **Shape** and changing the **Background Color** to white. If you can't make your mind up or want to use custom designed icons that are not available yet, that is possible. These icons can be changed later and I will show you how, later in the recipe.

12. Click on **Next** when you are happy with your launcher icons.

13. On the next screen make sure **Create Activity** is checked and change the selection from **BlankActivity** to **FullscreenActivity** as shown in the following screenshot:

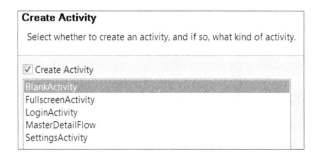

14. Click on **Next**.

15. On the next screen change the **Activity Name** to `MainActivity` and the **Layout Name** to `activity_main` as shown in the following screenshot. Be sure to make your capitalisation the same as shown in the following screenshot. What we are doing is giving Eclipse a few parameters to observe when it generates loads of code and settings for us in a moment.

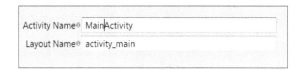

16. Click on **Finish**.

17. Eclipse does an awful lot of work for us. There are now literally dozens of files and folders ready prepared for us. We could even run the application on an Android phone with just a few more clicks. First let's wrap up our website in our app. In the left hand **Package Explorer** window double click on **layout** then double click on `activity_main.xml` as shown in the following screenshot:

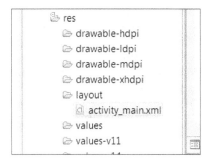

18. The `activity_main.xml` file describes the layout of our app. We are going to highlight a portion of code, delete it and replace it with our WebView code which will give us a browser like experience. At the moment we are in the **Graphical Layout** tab. We need to switch to the code layout. Find the `activity_main.xml` tab, highlighted in the following screenshot and click on it to switch to the code view.

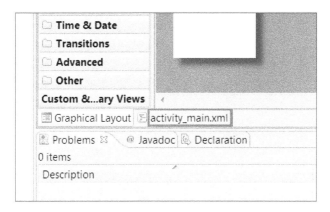

19. The code view looks like the following screenshot:

```xml
<RelativeLayout xmlns:android="http://schemas.android.com/apk/res/andr
    xmlns:tools="http://schemas.android.com/tools"
    android:layout_width="match_parent"
    android:layout_height="match_parent"
    tools:context=".MainActivity" >

    <TextView
        android:layout_width="wrap_content"
        android:layout_height="wrap_content"
        android:layout_centerHorizontal="true"
        android:layout_centerVertical="true"
        android:text="@string/hello_world" />

</RelativeLayout>
```

Graphical Layout | activity_main.xml

20. We should now see the code layout (pictured in the preceding screenshot). Within the code layout by using the scroll bar to the right, identify and highlight the block of code starting with `<TextView` and finishing with the first `/>` The following screenshot should help:

```
<TextView
        android:layout_width="wrap_content"
        android:layout_height="wrap_content"
        android:layout_centerHorizontal="true"
        android:layout_centerVertical="true"
        android:text="@string/hello_world" />
```

21. Highlight it by clicking, holding, and dragging. You should now have the following screenshot:

```
    tools:context=".MainActivity" >

    <TextView
            android:layout_width="wrap_content"
            android:layout_height="wrap_content"
            android:layout_centerHorizontal="true"
            android:layout_centerVertical="true"
            android:text="@string/hello_world" />

</RelativeLayout>
```

22. Press the *Delete* key on your keyboard and enter the following code or copy and paste from the file: `09_wrapping_our_site_in_an_android_web_view_activity_main.xml` available in the books download section on the Packt Publishing website.

```
<WebView  xmlns:android="http://schemas.android.com/apk/res/
android"
    android:id="@+id/webView"
    android:layout_width="fill_parent"
    android:layout_height="fill_parent"
/>
```

23. Click on **File** | **Save** to save our progress.

24. Now we have placed a WebView in our app. Time to make it work with a little bit of Java. In the **Project Explorer** window on the left, double click on **src**. Then double click on **com.hadronwebdesign.hadrondesign** (or whatever you named your package) and double click on `MainActivity.java` as shown in the following screenshot:

25. We can now see the main code that will make our app work. Find the line of code:

```
setContentView(R.layout.activity_main);
```

26. Put your cursor immediately after the semicolon **;** press *Enter* on the keyboard a few times to make some space between the above line and the next curly bracket **}**. It should look something like the following screenshot:

```
@Override
protected void onCreate(Bundle savedInstanceState) {
    super.onCreate(savedInstanceState);
    setContentView(R.layout.activity_main);



    SPACE


}
```

27. In the space you just created enter the following code or copy and paste it from `09_wrapping_our_site_in_an_android_web_view_MainActivity.java`.

```
webView = (WebView) findViewById(R.id.webView);
    webView.getSettings().setJavaScriptEnabled(true);
webView.loadUrl("http://www.joomla25.hadronwebdesign.co.uk");
```

28. Replace **www.joomla25.hadronwebdesign.co.uk** with your website URL.

29. You will notice that some of the code is underlined in red. We will fix this now. Near the top of this code window, find the following line of code:

```
public class MainActivity extends Activity {
```

30. Make a bit of space underneath this code like we did in step 23 and then enter the following line of code:

```
WebView webView;
```

31. Now hover your cursor over the text **WebView** that is underlined in red. The page will look like the following screenshot:

32. Select the first option **Import 'WebView' (android.webkit)**. Now all our errors are gone.

33. Click on **File | Save**.

34. One last step. In the **Package Explorer** window scroll to near the bottom and double click on **AndroidManifest.xml**. Select the tab labeled **AndroidManifest.xml** to bring up the code view of this file.

35. Find the line **<application** and immediately before it copy the following code or copy paste it from the file `09_wrapping_our_site_in_an_android_web_view_ activity_AndroidManifest.xml` available in the books download section on the Packt Publishing website.

```
<uses-permission android:name="android.permission.INTERNET" />
```

36. Click on **File | Save**.

How it works...

That was quite a tough one but it will never be as tricky as that again. Now we have the basics of a working Android app we can just copy, paste, add files, and edit to add functionality.

In this recipe we created a new Android project, defined its launcher icons, had Eclipse generate the project files and some starter code and then added our own code to wrap our site in the app. The last thing we did was to make any future users of our app aware that it will access the Internet. Without this line that we typed into the **AndroidManifest.xml** file the app will not be able to load our website.

See also

▸ The *Testing our app on the emulator* recipe

Testing our app on the emulator

At the end of each of the remaining recipes of this chapter you will have a working app with new functionality. This recipe tells us how to quickly test it on the emulator.

Getting ready

Have your current project open in Eclipse and read on.

How to do it...

You can follow these steps every time you want to test your app. Remember not to close the emulator when you're done if you think you will need it again soon. This will save you from the wait of loading it up every time.

1. From the Eclipse main menu select **Project** | **Clean**. Click on **OK** in the next pop up box.

2. To run the app find the little green and white play icon below the main menu bar as shown in the following screenshot:

3. Click on the play icon.

4. Select **Android Application** as shown in the following screenshot:

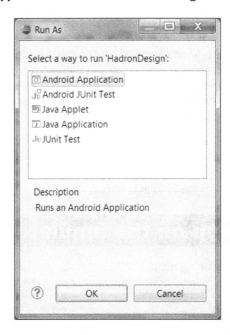

5. Click on **OK**.

6. You might be prompted to select an emulator. Simply double click on the emulator we created in the *Configuring an Android emulator (AVD)* recipe. Make a coffee or read a book while waiting for the emulator to start. I did say it was slow.

7. When the emulator has loaded, simulate a finger swipe on the bottom of the screen by single left clicking and dragging. Our new app will start automatically.

How it works...

Cleaning the project simply makes Eclipse refresh and re-link all aspects of the project. It is not always necessary but is good practice to avoid baffling errors from time to time.

The following screenshot displays what my test site from the previous recipe looks like in the emulator:

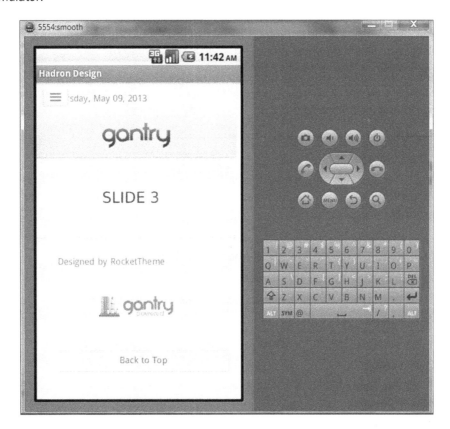

Exporting our app to use it on a real Android device

This quick recipe, like the last one will show us how to create the native Android `.apk` file which we can install on an Android device or upload to Google Play. We are looking at this now so that you can view it on a real Android device.

Getting ready

How you transfer files to an Android device differs from device to device, so to keep things easy to replicate across multiple different devices I suggest you create a free Dropbox account and install the free Dropbox app on any of the devices you want to run your app on. But any way you can transfer a file to your phone will suffice.

Set up Dropbox by visiting `www.dropbox.com` on your PC and searching for it and installing it from Google Play on your Android device.

How to do it...

First of all we need to make our phones accept apps that are not from Google Play. Obviously, when your app is published your users will not need to perform step 1 when getting it direct from Google Play.

1. Each Android device will vary slightly but it goes like this. **Menu | Settings | Security | Unknown sources (Allow Installation of non-Market apps)**.

2. Back to Eclipse. Select **File | Export**.

3. In the pop up box choose **Android | Export Android Application**.

4. Click on **Next**.

5. In the next box click on the **Browse** button and select your project.

6. Click on **Next**.

7. In the **File Name** field type a name for your Android application file. Choose **HadronDesign**.

8. Now we need to create a keystore, which is security measure. Select the **Create new keystore** radio button. For **Location** browse to somewhere memorable to keep your keystore. Let's choose `My Documents` as the folder and `keys` as the file name. Enter a password and then confirm the password. The page will look like the following screenshot:

9. Click on **Next**.

10. The next form is long but self explanatory. The only field to think about is the first one. **Alias**. Here it is simply entered `MyAlias`. You could treat this field a bit like a password hint field. What you put in here is arbitrary however. Here is the form all filled out. You will not need this step the next time you export your app. The page will look like the following screenshot:

11. Click on **Next**.

12. Click on **Browse** to choose were to put the finished, ready to deploy Android file. Here it is chosen as Desktop.

13. Now click on **Finish**.

14. On your desktop the `.apk` file will look like a `.zip` file. Open your Dropbox folder and drag it in as shown in the following screenshot:

15. Grab your Android device, start the Dropbox app and click on the file you just uploaded.

16. On your device press **Install** then **Open**.

How it works...

The process we went through is everything that is needed to create a working `.apk` file which is the Android app file format. The app can be installed directly onto an Android device as long as we complete step 1 first or is ready to be published on Google Play.

See also

▶ The *Publishing our app on Google Play* recipe

Branding our WebView

Now we are going to make our app, well, more app like. We will add a logo to the bottom of the screen. This will make our app look and feel more like something you would download from Google Play (which it will be) and less like something you simply browse to on the web.

Getting ready

Have ready a small logo perhaps no more than 300 pixels wide and 100 pixels high. Name it `logo.png`.

How to do it...

This is nice and easy, follow along carefully and we will soon be done.

1. In the Eclipse **Package Explorer** find and double click on the folder `drawable-mdpi`. Make the Eclipse window smaller and drag your logo file into `drawable-mdpi`. Your graphics are now ready to use.

 Do you see the file `ic_launcher.png`? This is the file you need to change if you want to update your launcher icons, perhaps because they weren't ready when we created them. In fact, notice the first four sub folders in the `Res` folder which `drawable-mdpi` is in. They are `drawable-hdpi`, `drawable-ldpi`, `drawable-mdpi`, and `drawable-xhdpi`. With any graphic that you use in your Android app (such as `ic_launcher.png` and `logo.png`) you can add multiple versions of the same file. This is so that you can supply higher resolution files for tablets and so on, and lower resolution for say phones with small screens. Android will then know which is the best image to use on any device. Exactly how to cater for this is beyond the scope of this recipe but you can find out more at `http://developer.android.com/guide/practices/screens_support.html`.

2. Now to add the image to our layout file, click on the **activity_main.xml** tab above the Eclipse code window. Just before the following line:

```
</RelativeLayout>
```

3. Add this code or, as usual, copy it from the code download from the Packt Publishing website download. The file is called `09_branding_our_webview_activity_layout.xml`.

```
<ImageView
android:id="@+id/imageView1"
android:layout_width="fill_parent"
android:layout_height="wrap_content"
android:src="@drawable/logo"
android:layout_alignParentBottom="true"/>
```

4. Click on **File** | **Save**.

How it works...

One quick edit to our layout file and we have a logo on our app. The following screenshot displays what it looks like in the emulator:

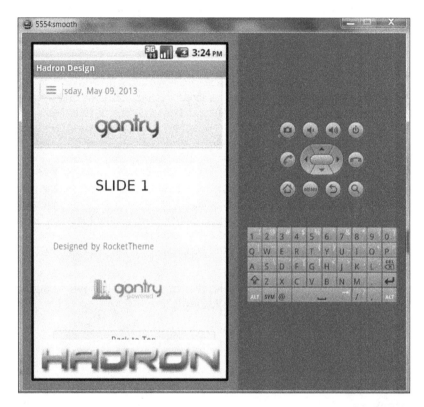

Publishing our app on Google Play

I have run out of space to show you how to add cool features. It is worth pointing out that you can fairly trivially do things like hide external links to make it even less like a website. You can add clicks to make the links more like buttons, swish page animations in between pages, and add Android menu items to important parts of your store like contact us or a special offers page.

All these features and more can be added by modifying the base app you have created in this chapter.

Now though, let's quickly publish the app so it is available for download from Google Play.

Getting ready

Export the latest version of your app using the *Exporting our app to use it on a real Android device* recipe.

Next head over to `http://developer.android.com/index.html` click on **Distribute** and sign up for a developer account. This will cost you $25. When you are ready read on.

Also prepare a few screenshots of your app ready to upload in a minute.

How to do it...

Log in to your account at `http://developer.android.com/index.html`.

1. At the top of the page in your developer console, click on the **+ Add New application** button as shown in the following screenshot:

2. Choose the **Default language*** and enter a **Title*** as shown in the following screenshot:

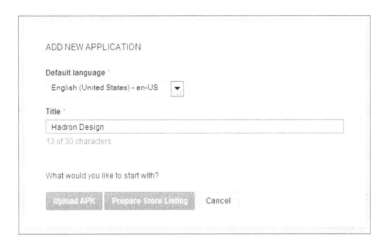

3. Click on **Upload APK**.
4. Click on **Upload your first APK**.
5. Click on the **Browse** button and select your apps `.apk` file.

6. Now click on the **Store Listing** tab on the left hand side as shown in the following screenshot:

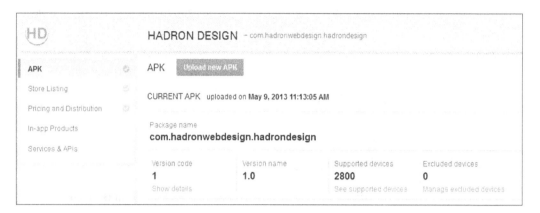

7. This is a fairly lengthy page but there is nothing awkward about it. Enter your full description in the **Description** field.

8. In the **Promo Text** field write a very short, very snappy, and enticing description of your app.

9. In the **Graphic Assets** section click on the **Add Image** button and select an image of your app in action.

10. Repeat step 9 for all of your images.

11. In the **Application Type** dropdown choose **Application**.

12. In the **Select a Category** dropdown choose **Shopping**.

13. In the **Select a Content Rating** dropdown choose **Everyone**, unless your site has an adult theme.

14. Now enter your website URL in the **Website** field.

15. Add a link to your privacy policy or select the radio button next to the label **Not submitting a privacy URL at this time**.

16. Be sure to click on **Save** at the top of the screen.

17. Click on the **Pricing and Distribution** tab on the left.

18. Click on the **Free** button.

19. Select all the countries you want your app to be shown in.

20. And click on the last two checkboxes on the list as shown in the following screenshot:

21. Click on **Save** at the top of the page.

22. In the top right hand corner of the page click on the **Draft** button. Choose **Published**. You are done!

How it works...

By uploading the `.apk` file and filling out all the blanks on the form we have made your app available on Google Play. It will probably take somewhere between an hour and a week to turn up in search results.

Keep adding features to your app and updating it on Google Play. Google will notice that you are adding to and improving your app and might reward you greater exposure.

Apps, VirtueMart, and Joomla! Resources

Apps

Turn your website content into an app! Refer to the following website:

`www.hadronwebdesign.com`

The preceding website makes bespoke Android apps based on your content.

VirtueMart templates

Here are some of the resources for VirtueMart templates:

Paid themes

Following are some of the websites which provide VirtueMart templates and themes at reasonable prices:

- `http://www.virtuemarttemplates.net`

    This website contains probably some of the nicest VirtueMart templates at extremely reasonable prices.

- `http://www.yagendoo.com`

  This website contains a good selection of simple but effective themes for VirtueMart as well as some other Joomla! e-commerce extensions like JoomShopping.

- `http://www.cmsmart.net`

  This website contains some very high quality VirtueMart templates available through their template club.

Free themes

The free themes will be available at `http://www.linelab.org/demo-templates-joomla/`

This website contains a small but nice quality selection of free themes.

Joomla! templates

Following are some of the resources for Joomla! templates:

Paid templates

Following are some of the websites where you would get themes and widgets at reasonable prices:

- `www.yootheme.com`

  This website contains really nice themes and super cool widgets as well.

- `www.rockettheme.com`

  This website contains some more really nice themes and cool widgets.

Free templates

The free templates are available at `http://www.jm-experts.com/free-joomla-extensions`.

These well designed templates also use the Gantry framework and are very neat!

Custom made templates

Custom made templates are available at `www.hadronwebdesign.com`.

VirtueMart extensions

The VirtueMart extensions are available at `http://www.cmsmart.net`.

It contains a wide range of VirtueMart related extensions including JomSocial, order management, and one page checkout.

Index

Thank you for buying
Building E-commerce sites with VirtueMart Cookbook

About Packt Publishing

Packt, pronounced 'packed', published its first book "*Mastering phpMyAdmin for Effective MySQL Management*" in April 2004 and subsequently continued to specialize in publishing highly focused books on specific technologies and solutions.

Our books and publications share the experiences of your fellow IT professionals in adapting and customizing today's systems, applications, and frameworks. Our solution based books give you the knowledge and power to customize the software and technologies you're using to get the job done. Packt books are more specific and less general than the IT books you have seen in the past. Our unique business model allows us to bring you more focused information, giving you more of what you need to know, and less of what you don't.

Packt is a modern, yet unique publishing company, which focuses on producing quality, cutting-edge books for communities of developers, administrators, and newbies alike. For more information, please visit our website: www.packtpub.com.

About Packt Open Source

In 2010, Packt launched two new brands, Packt Open Source and Packt Enterprise, in order to continue its focus on specialization. This book is part of the Packt Open Source brand, home to books published on software built around Open Source licences, and offering information to anybody from advanced developers to budding web designers. The Open Source brand also runs Packt's Open Source Royalty Scheme, by which Packt gives a royalty to each Open Source project about whose software a book is sold.

Writing for Packt

We welcome all inquiries from people who are interested in authoring. Book proposals should be sent to author@packtpub.com. If your book idea is still at an early stage and you would like to discuss it first before writing a formal book proposal, contact us; one of our commissioning editors will get in touch with you.

We're not just looking for published authors; if you have strong technical skills but no writing experience, our experienced editors can help you develop a writing career, or simply get some additional reward for your expertise.

Magento Beginner's Guide 2nd Edition

ISBN: 978-1-78216-270-4   Paperback: 320 pages

Learn how to create fully featured, attractive online stores with the most powerful open source e-commerce solution

1. Install, configure, and manage your own e-commerce store

2. Extend and customize your store to reflect your brand and personality

3. Handle tax, shipping, and custom orders

Building e-commerce Sites with Drupal Commerce Cookbook

ISBN: 978-1-78216-122-6   Paperback: 266 pages

Over 50 recipes to help you build beautiful, responsive eCommerce sites with Drupal Commerce

1. Learn how to build attractive eCommerce sites with Drupal Commerce

2. Customise your Drupal Commerce store for maximum impact

3. Reviewed by the creators of Drupal Commerce: The CommerceGuys

Please check **www.PacktPub.com** for information on our titles

PrestaShop 1.5 Beginner's Guide

ISBN: 978-1-78216-106–6   Paperback: 260 pages

Build your own attractive online store with this fast and flexible e-commerce solution

1. Build a fully featured, attractive online shop with PrestaShop

2. Add and customize your shop's products

3. Make more money by offering shipping and payment options to your site

Getting Started with nopCommerce

ISBN: 978-1-78216-644-3   Paperback: 134 pages

An in-depth, practical guide to getting your first e-commerce website up and running using nopCommerce

1. Learn to install and configure nopCommerce in order to start selling products online

2. Discover the key areas and features to get up and running fast

3. Learn how to create and manage products, shipping, and payment methods

Please check **www.PacktPub.com** for information on our titles